MULTIPLAN™ USER'S GUIDE

Erwin Schneider

JOHN WILEY & SONS
Chichester · New York · Brisbane · Toronto · Singapore

Library of Congress Cataloging in Publication Data:

Schneider, Erwin.
    Multiplan^{TM} User's guide.

    Includes index.
    1. Multiplan (Computer program)   I. Title.
HF5548.4.M74S36 1984   001.64'25   84-13037
ISBN 0 471 90565 8

British Library Cataloguing in Publication Data:

Schneider, Erwin.
    Multiplan^{TM} users' guide.
    1. Multiplan (Computer program)
    2. Business—Data processing
    I. Title
    658'.05425   HF5548.4.M

    ISBN 0 471 90565 8

Typeset by Pintail Studios, Ringwood, Hampshire
and printed by The Pitman Press, Bath, Avon.

ACKNOWLEDGEMENTS

Multiplan is a trademark of Microsoft Corporation.

The IBM Personal Computer (PC) is a trademark of International Business Machines.

VisiCalc is a trademark of VisiCorp, Inc.

Epson is a trademark of Epson Corporation.

This book has been written using the Multimate Word Processing Package created by SoftWord Systems, Inc. using a Hyperion Micro Computer, manufactured by Bytec Comterm Inc., Hyperion Division.

CONTENTS

INTRODUCTION
ABOUT THIS BOOK

I decided to write this book when I realized that Multiplan is seriously undervalued. I wrote it primarily for the very people that this product is most intended to serve, professional people who have no computer knowledge and no wish to obtain it.

Anyone who purchases Multiplan will obtain a manual supplied with the product. These manuals are very similar to each other, but have local variations to allow for the different computers on which it runs. While teaching Multiplan to business people I read quite a number of these manuals and became aware of the need for something different.

The manuals have a really useful training section. The reference section is usually very thorough. But there is a mental barrier between the way that most people think and the way that Multiplan works. The purpose of this book is to overcome this barrier.

The book is divided into four parts:

PART 1   The Multiplan Environment: What it is and how it fits into the range of solutions available on your computer.

PART 2   Major Themes in Multiplan: in-depth analysis of the topics for which people require help.

PART 3   Full Reference Guide: each command and sub-command has separate treatment in an easy-to-find format.

PART 4   Quick Reference Guide: all the technical terms used in Multiplan are clearly explained in a special section.

The structure of the book is especially designed to help people who have no wish to read it from start to finish: just to look up something and then get back to their computer.

Who should read this book?

The answer to this question is almost the same as 'Who should use Multiplan?'. Almost but not quite: it's perfectly possible to read the book and decide that Multiplan is not for you. Indeed there is a section which identifies the limitations that this product possesses. If it's those things you want to do then it's better to quit now and start looking for some other way of achieving those particular objectives.

Who would want to use Multiplan?

This book is intended for the potential users of Multiplan, who are to be found among the following:

* Executives in medium to large corporations with responsibility for planning and/or decision making.
* Proprietors of small businesses who need a 'thinking calculator' to help them achieve their business objectives.
* Self-employed professional people who want a computer capability to back up the service they provide for their clients, but none of this must be allowed to stop them being 100 per cent committed to their own professions. Multiplan isn't supposed to turn them into computer people: it should be a servant, not a master.
* Accountants and financial executives who need something better than a calculator to help them with their routine desk work.
* Engineers who need a responsive calculating and record-keeping aid which does not involve a big programming budget every time something new comes up on the horizon.
* Computer people who will quickly appreciate what a very good deal they're getting when they use a product of this power and ease of use.

The real reason for reading this book is to take advantage for yourself of what Multiplan can do to further your own work ambitions. If it can help you—and it very probably can—then you really ought to read this book.

What's new about this book?

This book is based on experience of helping people to use Multiplan. You'll find that it talks your language. Where there is a choice between using the language of the computer expert and of the non-computer person, there's no doubt about which wording has been chosen. The non-computer person is given preference every time. Many people feel that both the manual and the messages that appear in response to the HELP commands are too heavily biassed in favor of the computer people. In this book we're going to reverse that bias.

How to use this book

You will be using this book selectively. This means that there is no point in reading it from page one through to the last page. It certainly wasn't intended to be read in that way. The intention is that you can find quickly what you are looking for. This has meant that there is some repetition in the book. The purpose of that repetition is to try to present you with relevant information wherever you need it. What you'll be doing is to look at the contents list and deciding which parts you'll be wanting to read. Some general points of advice are included here but you'll be deciding for yourself before long.

PART 1   THE MULTIPLAN ENVIRONMENT

Go to this part for a Refresher Course, reminding you of the main rules of Multiplan. Look here also for some discussion of the use of Multiplan in the environment of your computer and some general hints.

PART 2   MAJOR THEMES IN MULTIPLAN

Look to this part to explain major topics such as printing or linking worksheets to each other. Here you will find much advice about the use of Multiplan.

PART 3   FULL REFERENCE GUIDE

Here you will find a structured account of each command and sub-command. Each command has two pages devoted to it: 'What it does' and 'How to use it'. Each sub-command has at least one page 'How to use it' and several have an extra page of 'Illustrated Examples'.

PART 4   QUICK REFERENCE GUIDE

Every technical term used in Multiplan is explained here. You can always refer to this part if you're not sure about some term used either in this book, or your manufacturer's manual, or on the Multiplan screen. Some words are just defined and in those cases the Quick Reference Guide acts as a Glossary. In the other cases there are two entries: you'll find both a simple explanation at the level of a Glossary and an advanced explanation of the word in the context of Multiplan.

The Reference Guides

You'll often find no need to go beyond the Quick Reference Guide and the Full Reference Guide. They're both designed for easy access and appear in a distinctive part of the book.

Conclusion

Don't let the size and the structure of the book discourage you from either using Multiplan or reading this book! Both are simpler to use than you realize by just reading this. The best way to find out is by trying.

When you have really got into the Multiplan way of working and thinking you'll find that you'll know what to do without thinking about it. You don't swim while thinking about it all the time. First you learn to swim, but after that you do it without thinking about it. It's the same with Multiplan. As you improve you'll need this book less and less. When you don't need it at all, then you'll really know it's been successful!

PART 1

THE MULTIPLAN ENVIRONMENT

Introduction

In this part we will be looking at the general environment of Multiplan. In particular we have a section which gives you a chance to refresh your memory about Multiplan. It doesn't seek to duplicate what is available in your manufacturer's manual. It gives you a chance to find out quickly what the main features of Multiplan are. Then you will be able to get full benefit from the rest of the book.

The full list of topics covered is as follows:

WHAT IS MULTIPLAN?

Introduction

There are two important questions to ask about Multiplan. They are:

1. What is it?
2. How do you use it?

We'll wait a moment before talking about the second question—after all that's what the entire book is about. But first we'll consider what it really is.

General definition

Multiplan is an executive tool. It lets you harness the potential of your computer without putting you into the power of the computer experts. It takes the tedium out of routine pencil and paper operations. Whenever you get out a piece of paper and develop your information with frequent changes, especially with frequent use of an eraser, then you have a use for Multiplan.

Types of user

It's easier to expand on this theme when addressing a particular kind of user. There seems to be *three* of those:

1. The **Professional User** who understands the application and is using the computer and its software as a tool to assist in his or her work.
2. The **Clerical User** who carries out the instructions of the Professional User but does not decide what Multiplan will do.
3. The **Computer Specialist** who wants to place Multiplan within the total range of computer solutions available.

Depending on which of these categories describes, or most closely describes, your position you will find a section below to help you understand what Multiplan has to offer.

For the professional user

Most professional people have a strong intuitive feel about what they expect a computer to do for them. It shouldn't get in the way: it should be a support, particularly in the areas of planning, evaluation of alternative strategies and remembering previous solutions which have been discarded on the way. It should have a record of how you reached each alternative solution. I am confident that you will find that Multiplan can provide all these facilities for you. You may well find yourself agreeing with the user who said that it is everything that a calculator ought to be, but isn't. Until quite recently such a thing was just not possible on a computer.

You will also welcome the fact that you are not going to be dependent on other people, notably in the Computer Department, to get your work done. You'll probably get the work done on a low cost microcomputer, either in your own office (or not very far away from it) or in your home.

If you are very obsessive, and many professional people are, then you won't want to tear yourself away from the process of using Multiplan. However the entering of data, once the structure has been correctly set up, can be a very time-consuming task. So it is feasible for the professional to set the job up and then leave the routine processing to be done by a clerical assistant.

One final distinction which, although obvious, justifies a place here. Multiplan does not *do* anything. Unlike a payroll program, or an invoicing package, it simply waits to be told what to do. A homely little analogy: in a train or an airplane you go where you are taken. In an automobile you are in the driver's seat: you decide where you are going with Multiplan.

For the clerical assistant

Multiplan is not going to look very different to you from most jobs on a computer. You'll still be entering information, such as lists of sales figures or client information, at the keyboard. You'll probably be printing out the results.

One thing that will seem a bit different is that you tend to see more than just what you are entering: you may well see the results as well. That won't matter as long as you have a clear understanding of what you are expected to do, preferably in writing. If no one gives you that: take my advice and ask! As for making mistakes, you can always go back and put it right. There should be no danger of you accidentally destroying valuable data since use should have been made of the LOCK facility before you started.

Be quite sure that you cannot damage Multiplan itself whatever you do. At the worst you can lose your data, but the computer and Multiplan are quite safe. One thing you should be aware of: the diskettes that you use *are* fragile. Take very seriously the advice on the labels about not bending them or spilling coffee on them.

For the computer specialist

Multiplan is neither a programming language nor an application package. It belongs to that class of software which enables people to get things done without programming. There are various fancy words being used for this kind of thing: application generator is just one example. In practice none of that matters very much; just consider what you can do.

In computing terms Multiplan enables people to:

* Work in arrays of rows and columns which can be given any significance the user wishes.
* Use powerful copying facilities for quickly building up the worksheet.
* Enter formulas, which cause the results to be displayed in the position where each formula appears.
* Make numerous and major changes to the worksheet such as the insertion and deletion of any parts with automatic recalculation of addresses.
* Link up different worksheets to each other to achieve powerful summarization and consolidation capabilities.
* Use the LOCK facility which enables the originator of the worksheet to protect the formulas from being accidentally destroyed.

Through a user friendly menu system the user is helped to create worksheets without any computer knowledge. Diagnostics appear at the time when they are needed. A range of functions, rather like those that are available to the BASIC programmer, is provided. Results can be instantly verified at the screen. In practice many people with absolutely no computer experience have successfully performed significant work on their computers using Multiplan without the need for any specialist assistance.

Application ideas

Another way of presenting the subject is to list some of the applications for which Multiplan has been used. This may give you some ideas about what you might achieve for yourself. The list, which is certainly *not* meant to exclude things which happen not to get mentioned, includes the following applications:

Checking a Bank Statement;
Keeping a Price List up to date;
Keeping a Product List up to date;
Investment Appraisal;
Energy Management;
Administering Salary Reviews;
Preparing Quotations;
Calculating Sales Commissions;
Applying Quantity/Product Discounts;
Forecasting Material Requirements for a Production Schedule;
Maintaining an Inventory of Goods in Stock and pricing them;
Putting through a Price Change;
Consolidating intercompany plans or schedules;

International currency calculations;
Brokerage Calculations;
Cash-flow Calculations;
Internal Rate of Return Calculations;
Comparing different Loan Repayment Schedules.

Conclusion

You will probably have gathered that this list is almost infinitely extendable. There are very few limitations. They certainly include the capacity of your computer, whether you know the factors which go to solving your particular problem and the time needed to perform this task. But the biggest obstacle to using Multiplan to solve everyday problems is the need for imagination to see opportunities and to grasp them.

REFRESHER COURSE

Introduction

The purpose of this section is to give a logical account of Multiplan in as short a space as possible. You may want to read this chapter if you:

* Have already learned to use Multiplan but have not used it for some time: you won't want to repeat the lessons in your manufacturer's manual.
* Know some other spreadsheet system and wish now to move over to Multiplan.

The explanations are therefore brief. They will give you sufficient grounding to enable you to benefit from the rest of the book. If a slower approach is preferred you may wish to read the training part of your manufacturer's manual.

Ground to be covered

The ground to be covered is itemized immediately below this paragraph. Each aspect is covered in turn in order to build up a thorough grasp of Multiplan one step at a time. The Index of the book will emphasize references to this section, since when you want to look up something quickly this is one of the most important chapters available for that purpose.

THE WORKSHEET
> The Display Area
> The Control Area

HOW DATA IS REPRESENTED IN THE COMPUTER
> Numbers
> Text

FORMULAS

REFERENCING
  Absolute Referencing
  Relative Referencing
  Naming
  Ranges
  Intersections
  Unions

COMMANDS AND FUNCTIONS
  The 20 Commands
  The 36 Sub-commands
  The 42 Functions

Conventions used in this chapter

The points are made in a sequence which builds up an understanding from what has been explained before. The first mention of a point appears in **bold**, later ones will depend naturally on the first reference. (Just occasionally it's going to be necessary to mention something that has to be explained later: this will always appear in parentheses like this sentence.)

THE WORKSHEET

In Multiplan we work on a worksheet, also known as a **model** or a **spreadsheet**. These words all mean that we set out the information in a way that we can readily use and alter. The information is set out in a grid-like structure. We have complete freedom in deciding where we are going to put our information and where we want Multiplan to do its own work.

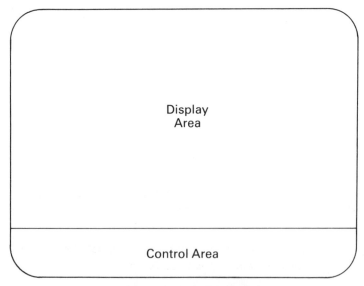

Display
Area

Control Area

Figure 1   Multiplan screen

Parts of a Screen

A Multiplan Screen is divided into two main parts:

1. The **display area**, which contains the top 20 lines of the screen.
2. The **control area**, which holds the bottom 4 lines of the screen.

The split is illustrated in Figure 1.

Display Area

The top part of the screen is known as the Display Area which is where the work-sheet is being developed. You can think of it as your window into as much of the worksheet as can be fitted into the screen. This is where you see the results of your actions. The display area is illustrated in Figure 2.

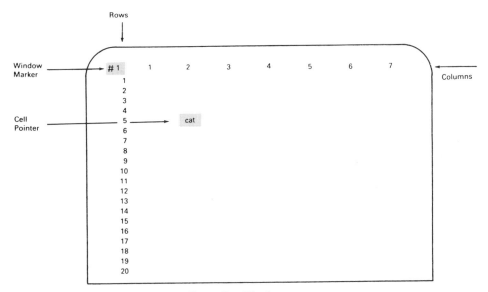

Figure 2   Display area

The contents are arranged in the form of **rows** and **columns**.

A row is a set of positions, into which we put information, which is arranged from left to right across the worksheet. There are 255 rows in a Multiplan worksheet.

A column is a set of positions, into which we put information, which is arranged from top to bottom down the worksheet. There are 63 columns in a Multiplan worksheet.

The place where a row and column meet is called a **cell**. You generally work on a cell. Some operations are made on a group of cells.

The cell that you are working on is called the **active cell**.

The active cell is emphasized for you by a **Cell Pointer**. This means that the cell is highlighted. The Cell Pointer will always be the same width as the cell to which it is pointing.

A Cell is identified by its row and column position: the cell that appears in the fourth row of the second column is known as R4C2. Note this sequence: in Multiplan rows *must* come before columns.

The display area also contains one or more **Window Markers** at the top left of each window. You can recognize them by the # sign followed by the window number, and they are also highlighted. They tell you which window number you are looking at. (The meaning of windows is discussed later on.) There is always at least one window in Multiplan, which is then known as Window #1.

Control Area

The bottom part of the screen is called the Control Area. This is where you make things happen. You use the Control Area to change the contents of the Display Area. The Control Area contains four lines. The Control Area is illustrated in Figure 3.

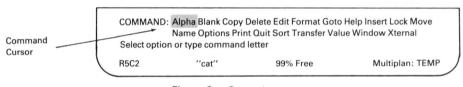

Command
Cursor

COMMAND: Alpha Blank Copy Delete Edit Format Goto Help Insert Lock Move
Name Options Print Quit Sort Transfer Value Window Xternal
Select option or type command letter

R5C2   ''cat''   99% Free   Multiplan: TEMP

Figure 3   Control area

The first two lines are called the **Command Lines**. These contain the 20 commands that enable you to build up your worksheet. Note that each begins with a different letter of the alphabet. One of the 20 commands is always highlighted by a **Command Cursor**.

NOTE CAREFULLY
There are *three* highlighted positions on the screen: the Cell Pointer and the Window Marker at the top, and the Command Cursor at the bottom.

You tell Multiplan what to do next by choosing a Command. You choose a command in one of two ways:

1. Pressing the space bar until the Command Cursor is highlighting the command that you wish to use, and then pressing 'enter'.
2. Pressing the alphabetic key on your keyboard which is the initial letter of the command that you require. For instance if the command you want is LOCK then you will just press 'L' and you will enter the LOCK command.

> **ADVICE** If you are familiar with the position of the keys on a keyboard you will be better off to press the initial letter. But if you are unfamiliar with a keyboard then you could waste time looking for the correct key to press and then the space-bar method will suit you better.

The third line of the Control Area is called the **message line**. This is used by Multiplan to tell you something: either what to do next or to advise you that you have done something wrong.

The fourth line of the Control Area is the **status line**. This provides a continuous view of what is gong on inside Multiplan. It tells you three things:

1. The identity of the active cell, followed by its contents.
2. The percentage of the memory still free, showing you all the time how much further you can go in building up this worksheet before you run out of space.
3. The worksheet name, that is the name of the current worksheet, which Multiplan needs to distinguish this one from the others that are being worked on.

HOW DATA IS REPRESENTED
INSIDE THE COMPUTER

To do any useful work we need a method of getting data into the computer and also a method of performing calculations.

In Multiplan data is described as **numeric** or **text**.

Numeric data

When the Cell Pointer is placed on a cell all we have to do is to press a numeric key for Multiplan to recognize that we wish that particular number to be held in that cell, the active cell. The full range of keys that achieve this objective is as follows:

$$0 \ 1 \ 2 \ 3 \ 4 \ 5 \ 6 \ 7 \ 8 \ 9 \ - \ + \ \char94 \ \% \ \$$$

For most purposes Multiplan will give you all the accuracy you need. The simplest way of showing that you have finished the entry of a piece of numeric data is to press 'Return'.

Text

Multiplan also allows us to enter **text**. This is defined as alphabetic type of information which is needed in a worksheet so that we can give descriptions to the data. (Text is going to be entered by the use of the ALPHA command, which is dealt with later.) Text has to fit into the width of the cell into which it is entered. Other manuals tend to refer to text as **strings** or **character strings**, but in this book we are satisfied to call it just text, which is what it is.

Formulas

We also have a method in Multiplan by which we can instruct the computer to perform the calculations that we want. These calculations are entered into the cells where we want the answer to appear. Such an entry is called, in Multiplan, a **formula**. A formula follows the natural rules of arithmetic which are easy to learn. (You will find them obvious if you already happen to know BASIC programming. You don't *need* to know programming, though.)

Rules for formulas

The simplest form of a formula operates on two numbers. If I enter into a cell the formula 12+2 I will get the result of 14. What I can also do is to refer to another cell in the formula. For instance:

R3C9	**R3C10**
127	R3C93*3

As soon as you have finished giving Multiplan its instruction you will get the answer of 381. The use of the '*' character to represent multiplication introduces this example of mathematical notation in Multiplan. Note that any time the contents of Row 3 Column 9 changes, so does the answer in Row 3 Column 10.

Note also that Row 3 Column 10 has *two* different characteristics. These are:

The Formula which remains the same until you change it; and

The Value, which changes every time the factors in the formula change, in this case Row 3 Column 9.

This is an important distinction: you will normally see the **value**, but this is only there because of the formula which you *don't* normally see. You can always see what the formula is by looking at the Status Line of the active cell.

REFERENCING

In order to give Multiplan its instructions it is necessary for cells to be **referred** to. You will use commands, acting on other cells and put the answer into the active cell. These other cells must be called something in a way that Multiplan can understand. We will be covering six different concepts in order to explain how Multiplan enables us to reference cells both easily and powerfully. These are:

Absolute Referencing
Relative Referencing
Naming
Ranges
Intersections
Unions

Absolute referencing

An absolute reference is calling a cell by its row and column number position. So if you enter R3C6, you have an absolute reference. This means the cell where the third row meets the sixth column. Note that the row must come first: you may *not* enter C6R3.

Relative referencing

In contrast to absolute referencing we have the concept of relative referencing. This means expressing the location of a cell not by its own row and column number but in terms of its relative position to where the active cell is at present. For example:

If the active cell is in R4C6 then relative to the active cell, R3C6 becomes R[−1]C.

This method of describing a reference works this way:

Row 3 is one less than Row 4, that is R[−1]. It means 'one row number less than the row number of the active cell'. Column 6 is the same in both the active cell and in the cell being referenced. It is neither plus or minus the current column. Therefore, in relative terms it is described as C. This means 'the same column number as the column number of the active cell'.

Two further examples:

If the active cell is in R10C20, then relative to it R19C2 is expressed as R[+9]C[−18].

If the active cell is R27C9, the reference to R27C10 relative to the active cell is RC[+1].

Reasons for relative referencing

Relative referencing is an important feature of Multiplan, the purpose of which is by no means to confuse people who wish to learn how to use it. The main advantage arises when we are copying formulas to other parts of the worksheet.

For example we have Gasoline in Column 2 and Electricity in Column 3 with the rows starting at Row 4 referring to different factories. In Row 4 Column 4 we have the formula +RC[−2]+RC[−1] giving Energy. Using the COPY command we copy down that actual formula to all the rows for which we have entries. The same formula is valid because it is all relative. This would not have worked if we had been using Absolute Referencing. This shows that in Multiplan relative referencing is more natural than absolute referencing.

The recommended way of entering references

You do *not* have to enter the relative references yourself at the keyboard. There is a much easier way. We needed to recognize these [+19] and [−47] symbols, because you will see them when Multiplan displays references to you. It will be your way of checking that what you put in is correct: but you need never enter either a relative or even an absolute reference. A useful analogy: it's much easier to read a foreign language than to write it.

Pointing

The easier way of entering references, both absolute and relative, is that of **pointing**. If the active cell is R3C6 then we refer to R4C6 relatively just by pointing the Cell Pointer to R4C6: this will be interpreted by Multiplan as R[+1]C. That is what you will see in the formula as it appears in the Status Line. No need for us to do the calculation. Multiplan will do it, and only provided that we point the Cell Pointer correctly, the answer is certain to be correct. To get an absolute reference we simply go through this procedure and then press the special **Function Key** called 'Reference' which in our recent example would convert the R[+1]C into R4C6.

You *need* to make a relative reference into an absolute reference when you do not want it recalculated to a new position when the formula is copied. In the Gasoline and Electricity example we may have wanted to multiply all our readings by a standard measure of thermal efficiency: if that had been in R1C1 we could have pointed to it in our formula in R4C4 and then made it absolute by using the Reference function key.

It is never *wrong* in Multiplan to form references, whether absolute or relative, and enter them in at the keyboard. They will be accepted, and provided they have been correctly calculated, will produce the correct results. But, you are advised that to try to do this is to deprive yourself of one of the main benefits of Multiplan.

ADVICE   Once you have mastered the technique of pointing you will find Multiplan quicker and easier to use.

Rows and columns

We can now consider another aspect of the design of Multiplan. Other spreadsheet systems often identify columns by letters and rows by numbers. Row 4 Column 6 would generally be called F4, since F is the sixth letter of the alphabet. Multiplan's superiority over this technique can be seen in the relativity calculation, which would be absurd with an alphabetic notation. Multiplan has been criticized by people who have not studied the product and complain at having to enter things like R190C52. This is not necessary and you are advised never to do this. There is always a better way.

Naming

In Multiplan we can give **names** to the elements that we use in our formulas and commands. A name can be used to represent a cell or group of cells. The reference will always be treated as though it was an absolute reference.

There are many advantages in the use of names. The chief one is that we can make our formulas more meaningful. It gets us further away from the 'unnatural' procedure of entering expressions like R[-9]C[+26]. To give that cell the name, for instance, 'Taxation' makes the task of developing the worksheet easier to manage. (More information on Naming is given on page 86.)

Ranges

You can save yourself time by performing the same operation on a whole group of cells. For instance, you might want to zeroize them all at once. You do this by:

* Pointing to the start of the range.
* Entering a colon.
* Pointing to the end of the range.
* Pressing 'Return'.

This method lays additional stress on the importance of pointing. We'll go through an actual example, illustrated in Figure 4.

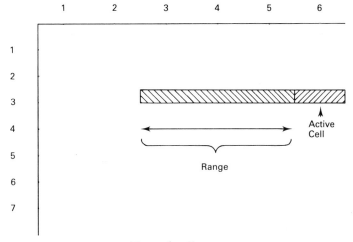

Figure 4   Range

If the active cell is Row 3 Column 6 and we want to blank out the three cells to the left, we go through the following operations:

* Make sure that the Cell Pointer is in Row 3 Column 6.
* Enter the command BLANK by pressing 'B'.
* Point three cells to the left, which is the beginning of the range.
* Enter a colon.
* Note that the Cell Pointer automatically moves back to the active cell (R3C6).
* Point one cell to the left, which is the end of the range.
* Press 'Return'.

We now have our range. (We'll be using it in the course of other operations that we haven't covered yet.) The status line displayed R3C3:R3C5 before we pressed 'Return'.

NOTE

You identify a range by means of a colon. It separates the start of the range from the end.

Possible shapes of a Range

A range always has a 'shape'. This shape is drawn in straight lines from the first reference (before the colon) and the second reference (after the colon). This gives you the shape of a rectangle, which has four sides. The four sides are built up by 'drawing' four lines to cover the shortest distance from the first reference to the second reference. Where they meet gives us our rectangle. See Figure 5.

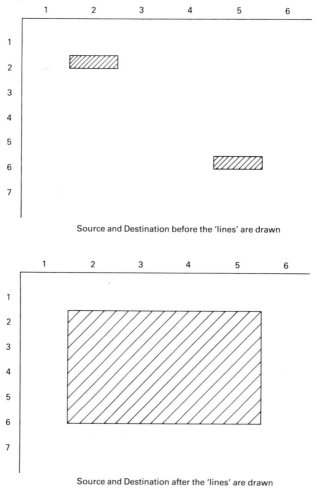

Source and Destination before the 'lines' are drawn

Source and Destination after the 'lines' are drawn

Figure 5   How the range R2C2 : R6C5 is 'drawn' by pointing to
the source, pressing colon and pointing to the destination

A range can be any one of the following:

A rectangle with the top wider than the side (as in the example above).
A rectangle with the side longer than the top.
Just one Column wide (for example R33:43C17).
Just one Row deep (for example R90C42:52).

INTERSECTIONS

An intersection is where rows and columns meet and have an area in common. The simplest of all Multiplan references, a single cell, is an intersection. R50C25 is the intersection of Row 50 and Column 25. The intersection may be between Rows 50 to 55 and Columns 25 to 30. Such an intersection would define an area for use with one of the commands. The way Multiplan recognizes this intersection is by the following:

R50:55C25:30

The colons represent ranges. When the R50:55 is placed alongside the C25:30 this represents an intersection. It is also true of a single cell reference. Our example was R50C25. See Figure 6.

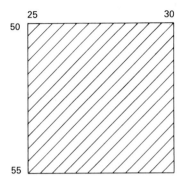

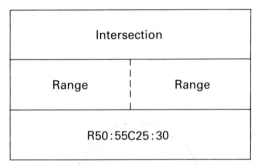

The area described as an intersection of ranges.
Multiplan prompts will appear like this:

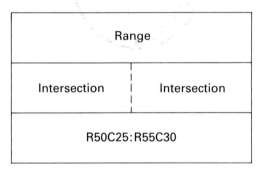

The same area described as a range of intersections.
You will use the pointing method in this way.

Figure 6   Ranges and intersections

If we had used a name as one of the references, which we may do, then a space should be left. For instance, we can enter 'north C25:30', so long as the name 'north' has been defined to be something like R50:55. The reason we have a space in the example is that Multiplan can detect the end of one reference and the beginning of the next. We need no space in 'R50:55C25:30' because the meaning is quite clear. R and C mean just 'Row' and 'Column'. (That is why we may not call a name either R or C.)

NOTE

You identify an intersection because the two elements in it are separated by *either* a space, if it is needed, *or* by nothing.

UNIONS

In addition to ranges and intersections we also have **Unions**. Unions are lists of things which are combined for a particular purpose. If you want to blank out three cells that are not adjacent you can do it as one operation by referencing, for instance,

R15C27,R18C27,R21C27

Please note that you can always blank each cell individually, but a union makes it quicker. Unions can also represent more complex shapes. R9,C2 is a valid union reference. It means 'both of Row 9 *and* Column 2'. If it had been an intersection (R9C2) it would have been a single cell. This example, though valid, is not likely to be of much use to you. Of greater value is the ability to reference a shape that is not an exact rectangle. If you look at Figure 7 you can see that a normal intersection of ranges cannot define it. But if we use a Union as well as an Intersection then we can achieve what we need.

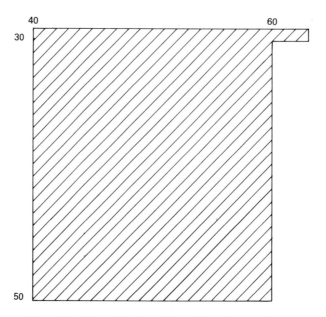

Figure 7   Example of a union with an intersection—
R30C40 : R50C60, R30C61

NOTE

You identify a union by the use of commas which separate items in the list.

REFERENCING IN GENERAL

We have now considered briefly the six different elements concerned with referencing. These can all be used in conjunction with each other. Here are some examples:

R13C19:Gas   Absolute, Name and Intersection
R[−2]C[+4],R1C1:R10C2   Relative, Absolute, Range, Intersection and Union

Note also two special kinds of reference: rows and columns. R27 or C19 are valid references to a whole row and column.

The choice is yours. These alternatives exist so that you can conveniently issue the commands you require.

COMMANDS IN GENERAL

We use these basic tools in commands which are issued from the Command Lines in the Control Area of the screen. You *must* be able to see the two lines of all the commands from ALPHA through to eXTERNAL before you can enter a command. If you do not have the two lines present you can cause them to come up on your screen by pressing 'Cancel'.

You have the ability to choose from any one of the 20 commands and, through them, any one of the 32 sub-commands. There is a standard approach which is common to commands in general. You enter the command, your Command Lines are replaced by a set of parameters which relate to this command. You *either* choose from a list of sub-commands *or* fill in the fields that now appear on the Command Lines, depending on whether the command has any sub-commands.

The structure of commands, sub-commands and fields is designed to make it easy for you to give the computer your instructions. In many cases you are prompted for the actual response you want to make. The details of these *proposed* responses are fully discussed in the Full Reference Guide.

The calculations are not directly performed by commands at all. To perform a calculation you enter VALUE (or '=' or a number of other characters) and then enter your formula.

Type of Command

Building up the Worksheet	ALPHA, VALUE, COPY, EDIT, FORMAT, NAME, LOCK
Manipulating the Worksheet's structure	INSERT, DELETE, MOVE
Using the Worksheet	GOTO, BLANK, SORT, WINDOW
Organizing a session	TRANSFER, OPTIONS, QUIT
Connecting different Worksheets	eXTERNAL
Printing the Result	PRINT
Getting help from Multiplan	HELP

The main purposes of these commands are:

Command	Purpose

Building up the Worksheet

ALPHA	Enters alpha text.
VALUE	Enters numeric values or formulas (but you can do that also by entering numbers or by entering '=').
COPY	Duplicates text and numbers, also copies formulas with the correct relative reference.
EDIT	Alters previously entered entries including numbers, text and formulas.
FORMAT	Gets the worksheet's displayed information into your preferred form.
NAME	Gives selected parts of your data a name that you can use in other commands.
LOCK	Protects selected parts of the worksheet from accidental loss.

Command	Purpose

Manipulating the Worksheet's Structure

INSERT	Opens up the Worksheet to make room for new cells that you wish to insert.
DELETE	Closes up the Worksheet to remove cells that you wish to remove.
MOVE	Changes over the position of rows or columns.

Using the Worksheet

GOTO	Quickly move around the Worksheet.
BLANK	Remove the contents of a cell or a group of cells.
SORT	Resequences the specified rows according to the contents of one of the columns in those rows.
WINDOW	Splits the screen into different areas for viewing non-adjacent parts of the worksheet.

Organizing a Session

TRANSFER	Makes important decisions such as loading and saving a worksheet.
OPTIONS	Performs a number of specialized tasks concerned with the running of your worksheet.
QUIT	Leave Multiplan and return to the control of your operating system.

Connecting Different Worksheets

eXTERNAL	Connects different worksheets together.

Printing the Results

PRINT	Prints the worksheet under your control.

Getting help from Multiplan

HELP	Multiplan helps you to understand its own rules.

FUNCTIONS

The 42 different functions provide a 'secondary' supply of operations in Multiplan. They're not so obvious. They don't appear on the Command Lines at any stage— there certainly wouldn't be any room. But they perform many useful tasks and they can make the construction of formulas a lighter task.

SUM

We'll find out about functions by looking at the one most commonly used: SUM. If the cells in R30C23:34 all have sales information over a period of 12 months it would be very lengthy to enter R30C23+R30C24+R30C25 . . ., even if we use the pointer. The function SUM does this much quicker. Just enter SUM(R30C23:R30C34), and you may use the pointer, and the effect is as though you had entered each month's reference separately. Note that to enter a Function you use the same procedure as when you enter a Formula: a Function really *is* a formula—one that Multiplan has prepared for you.

All the Functions

We'll also classify the functions in terms of their main purpose.

Arithmetic	SUM, MIN, MAX, AVERAGE, COUNT
Mathematical	NPV, STDEV, ABS, SQRT, MOD, PI, LN, LOG10
Data representation	NA, INT, ROUND, EXP
Logical	IF, ISNA, OR, AND, NOT, TRUE, FALSE, ISERROR
Text	VALUE, LEN, FIXED, REPT, DOLLAR, MID
Table	LOOKUP, INDEX
Geometric	ATAN, COS, SIN, TAN
Iterative	DELTA, ITERCNT
Miscellaneous	ROW, COLUMN, SIGN

Nesting Functions

Individual functions become more effective when used in combination with other functions. The process of combining functions is described as **nesting**, since one is placed inside another. Here are some examples:

Nested Functions	Meaning
SQRT(SUM(R20:40C12))	The square root of the sum of the cells in the range R20C12 to R40C12.
ROUND(AVERAGE(Checks),2))	The average of all the cells in the area named 'Checks', rounded to two decimals.
ABS(MIN(C15))	The absolute value (ignoring the negative sign, if any) of the smallest number in Column 15.

Note that in all cases of nested Functions there must be a balance of left and right parentheses. Failure to produce this balance will lead to a 'Error in Formula' message.

All Functions are followed by parentheses which may contain zero, one, two or three **arguments**. These arguments are additional pieces of information required, such as the area being summated, the number of decimals being rounded, etc. The arguments are always separated by commas.

Operators

In the course of supplying the formulas and the functions that go toward them you will use a number of different operators.

Symbol	Meaning	Where Used
+	Add	Formulas
–	Subtract	Formulas
*	Multiply	Formulas
/	Divide	Formulas
^	Exponentiation	Formulas
%	Percent	Formulas
.	Period	Formulas
&	Concatenator	Text Functions
( )	Parentheses	Formulas and Functions
>	Greater than	Logical operations
<	Less than	Logical operations
=	Equal to	Logical operations
,	Comma	Functions

CHECKLIST OF WHAT TO DO IN EVERY SESSION

Introduction

In keeping with other parts of this book, this section is intended for rapid reference. It will pay you to have a quick look here every time you go into a Multiplan session, until all the hints contained in this chapter become thoroughly familiar to you.

WHEN PLANNING A WORKSHEET

Rows and Columns

Decide what is to go into rows and what is to go into columns. Remember:

How you are going to print it: you can go on extending downwards more easily than to the right.
Sorting: you can sort on a column but not on a row.

Formats

Any defaults you could use?
Commas in FORMAT OPTIONS?

Space

Keep space down, remember the rectangle which fixes the memory which has been used up. Useful for speed!

Presentation

Get headings aligned with contents.
Use vertical and horizontal markers.
Use upper case.
Use spacings to 'balance' the worksheet.
(See Hints on Presentation, page 32.)

Make use of prototypes

Don't overwrite your only version with live data.
Make this your prototype.
LOAD the prototype to start a new account, add live data to SAVE it with a new name.

One large worksheet v. several small ones

Important to decide.
One large worksheet gets difficult to manage and is *slow*.
Several smaller worksheets are easier to maintain and change.

The simple 'trial' example

Don't enter all 65 departmental descriptions when you are still planning a worksheet. Put in just a few and be prepared to abandon your first effort. That way you won't have invested unnecessary effort. The 65 descriptions will be easy to enter when you have successfully developed your worksheet.

DURING EVERY DEVELOPMENT SESSION

Remember to SAVE after every session and every 20 minutes or so during a long session.

If you have a version which is pretty good and want to experiment with a new idea you're not too sure about but you don't want to lose what you've already got:

SAVE the old version using a filename of say TOTALS.
Try your new ideas and SAVE with the name of, say, TOTALS1.
You continue with several different ideas calling them TOTALS2 and TOTALS3, etc.

When you are satisfied with the solution you SAVE the final version as TOTALS and DELETE the others. This keeps your directory on the disk tidy.

Prototype your work: keep an entirely blank worksheet available. Every new accounting period you can LOAD the prototype and enter new data, saving it under a new name. That way you will always have your prototype free for use.

PROBLEMS IN UNDERSTANDING WHAT HAS GONE WRONG?

Enter FORMAT OPTIONS Formulas Yes: this will let you review all your formulas on the screen. This often shows some error in entering, editing or copying your formulas.

HANDING IT OVER AS A PROCESSING RUN

LOCK all your formulas.

Take advantage of the 'Next Unlocked Cell' key to guide your operator through the entry fields.

Leave the Cell Pointer in the right place when you SAVE the worksheet.

Help the operator to do the printing. If several areas need to be printed, it's easier if you name the, say, three areas 'A', 'B' and 'D'.

Give the operator good typed instructions which anticipate what will happen. Get the operator to do the first run with you watching.

COMMON PROBLEMS
AND HOW TO
OVERCOME THEM

Introduction

In this chapter we're going to look at a number of common problems that people encounter in their use of Multiplan. You'll find that what is being discussed is not the rules of Multiplan but merely the sort of thinking that is needed to take advantage of it. Experience of teaching Multiplan has shown that people welcome this material.

Breaking the range

You may suffer from unnecessary problems with a '#REF!' error message. Consider the following situation:

MONTH	AMOUNT
MARCH	139.06
APRIL	69.12
MAY	2854.94
JUNE	66.82
JULY	521.48
AUGUST	338.00
TOTAL	3989.42

This tabulation represents a moving six month total. When you are ready to enter the September figure and remove the March figure you might have a problem.

If in your SUM function you point to the 139.06, press 'Colon' and then point to the 338.00 you certainly do have a problem. If you INSERT September between August and the line of dashes above the total line the SUM will not include the September figure. (That is because September is outside the range that you set up in the SUM function.) Worse still when you DELETE March you will get a '#REF!' message. (That is because March was at one end of the range that was set up.) Many people believe that this is unavoidable and that you have to recreate the SUM function every time you need to make this kind of change.

The way to avoid this problem is as follows. Build the SUM function by pointing, not to March, but to the line of dashes above March, and not to August, but to the line of dashes below August. The dashes do not disturb the addition which ignores anything non-numeric. What does happen is that when you INSERT September and DELETE March, it causes no problem and we get no '#REF!' message. The reason is that the range is now larger than the area where the changes take place.

Prototyping

Another difficulty arises when you move from one time cycle, say an accounting period, to another. The narrative has already all been filled in and various linkages may have been set up if you have linked worksheets. The last thing you want to do at the start of a new accounting period is to 'tidy up' and rearrange your worksheet. You can avoid this kind of problem by using a prototype.

In a prototype there is no narrative filled in and the linkages, if any, are the 'standard' ones of your application. If the filename of your prototype is 'ACCPRO' then you can LOAD it at the start of a new accounting period, and then enter your narrative, etc. and SAVE it as, say, 'ACCJAN' or 'ACCFEB'. I've found it a good idea to 'label' my prototypes by putting some word in, say, R1C1 like 'PROTOTYPE'. This word I then alter in all the working copies.

Understanding your filenames

Unless you have a system to handle it, you'll be making up filenames whenever you're prompted for them in the TRANSFER SAVE sub-command. The problem then is remembering what they mean. This problem is solved if you build up your own naming conventions. A naming convention is just a useful way of naming things so that you know what you've got. Here's an example:

First three characters	Application
Next three characters	Time cycle

So you might have

ACCJAN	Meaning January Accounts
REC3RD	Meaning Receivables for third quarter
COMM84	Meaning the 1984 Commission Statement

Note that you don't *have* to use exactly six characters in the filename, but it will give your work a 'tidy' look if all the filenames are of a uniform length. Note also that you can easily fit a prototype into this convention:

INVPRO	Meaning a prototype inventory worksheet

'Large and unwieldy worksheets'

Multiplan builds up expectations of powerful systems. It is therefore not surprising that people build up very large and cumbersome relationships. The trouble is, they sometimes get themselves tied up in some really complex situations, and it may well not be Multiplan's fault!

Here are a few of the common symptoms and their suggested cures:

1. Putting too much into one worksheet: eXTERNAL COPY is a lot easier to handle than over-large worksheets!
2. Repeating many large parts of the worksheet so that you can display them alongside the results that refer to them: WINDOW does this for you.
3. Going into unnecessary detail: there is no point in going down to the sub-assembly level if you make no use of it. Planning the worksheet is desirable. It's seldom a good idea just to build it up without thinking about where you are going. I recommend a simple example with just a few representative entries, which you then discard when you are ready to build up the genuine worksheet.

'It takes too long'

Slow operations always give a computer system a bad name. As your ambitions grow so the amount of work you give Multiplan to do will also grow. More work always means more time. Even so, there are steps we can take to keep the time required to a reasonable minimum.

This is a list of tips, the most effective of which come earliest:

1. Turn recalculation off, using the OPTIONS command.
2. Keep the worlsheet as small as you can *reasonably* make it (don't compress it into so small a space that the presentation of the material suffers).
3. Forward references take longer to evaluate than backward references. SUM(R9:149C9) is evaluated more quickly in R150C9 than in R8C9.

Starting a new accounting period

You start a new accounting period by taking some of the figures from the old one. People often get stuck on how to do this. The problem is that what *was* the Carried Forward figure now becomes the Brought Forward figure. If you COPY the Carried Forward figure to the Brought Forward area, you will be COPYing the formula over, which will certainly be using the old Brought Forward Figure. This gets you an error message. But all you wanted to do was to take the **values** from the Carry Forward and place them in the Brought Forward field to start all over again.

Here is a picture of what we're trying to do:

DEPARTMENT	B/F	1ST QTR	2ND QTR	3RD QTR	4TH QTR	C/F
West	1,000	100	150	200	250	1,700
South	2,000	200	300	400	500	3,400
etc.						

We want to get the 1,700 from West's C/F to its B/F, and the 3,400 from South's C/F to its B/F. And we want to do it without losing the formula in the C/F column, which is the SUM of B/F, 1st qtr through to 4th qtr. If we COPY the cell with the 1,700 to the cell with the 1,000 we'll just get a '#REF!' message. Here's what we do instead.

We NAME the area where the 1,700 and the 3,400 are. We SAVE this worksheet, using a different filename, say YEAR01. We then name the worksheet again as, say, YEAR02. In the YEAR02 worksheet we now BLANK the whole area between the 1,000 and the 500.

At this stage the worksheet YEAR02 looks like this:

DEPARTMENT	B/F	1ST QTR	2ND QTR	3RD QTR	4TH QTR	C/F
West						0
South						0
etc.						

The C/F formulas are still intact, producing a correct answer of 0 every time.

We then enter an eXTERNAL COPY using the named C/F column from YEAR01 and take it into the B/F column. We choose to make this eXTERNAL COPY unlinked.

At this stage the worksheet YEAR02 looks like this:

DEPARTMENT	B/F	1ST QTR	2ND QTR	3RD QTR	4TH QTR	C/F
West	1,700					1,700
South	3,400					3,400
etc.						

The B/F cells in YEAR02 now contain the values of the C/F cells in YEAR01. The formula is still intact in the C/F column. YEAR02 is now waiting to have the different quarters' data entered. Thus we take the **values** and not the **formulas** by using eXTERNAL COPY. This is an example of another advantage of using the eXTERNAL command. Try it. It works.

USEFUL HINTS ON PRESENTATION

Introduction

In this section we will be looking at some ideas on how to use Multiplan more professionally. These aspects are not concerned with teaching you any of the rules of Multiplan which are all dealt with elsewhere in this book. What we'll be covering here is some ideas on how to make your worksheets appear more readable on the screen and on the printer.

Importance of presentation

When worksheets get printed out it is almost always in order to impress someone: either a client, a colleague or a boss. The impression we make with our reports can be caused easily as much by the report's appearance as by any of its contents. So it's worth while to find the time to give our worksheets a really professional appearance. Multiplan contains many features which enable us to improve the presentation and you are advised to consider the use of these features.

General hints

Consider the example on the page opposite (Figure 8). I don't claim that it is so perfect that you must imitate all its details. But it does contain some features that you might want to consider using in your own worksheets.

* All main headings appear in upper case. This makes them stand out.
* The title of the whole worksheet is emphasized by entering it with a blank space between all the letters. It was entered using the 'Cont' Format Code. It was centered by editing it.
* Horizontal and vertical marks give the page a 'completed' look.
* The vertical marks have been produced by having two columns at each side of the worksheet with a width of only three character positions. On the left the cells all contain ' |' and on the right they all contain '|
* The headings of the narrative column line up with the contents: they are all left justified.
* The headings of the other columns are right justified to match the numeric contents, but a single space has been placed at the right by using the edit keys.

```
--------------------------------------------------------------------------------
|                        C A S H - F L O W   F O R E C A S T                     |
|                                                                                |
|------------------------------------------------------------------------------- |
|                JANUARY     FEBRUARY      MARCH        APRIL        MAY       JUNE|
|--------------------------------------------------------------------------------|
|EXPENDITURE                                                                     |
|                                                                                |
|Opening Stock     $90,000.00  $86,200.00  $81,100.00  $76,400.00  $69,100.00  $61,475.00 |
|Purchases this mth $13,750.00  $13,750.00  $15,125.00  $15,125.00  $15,125.00  $57,200.00 |
|Sales this month  $17,550.00  $18,850.00  $19,825.00  $22,425.00  $22,750.00  $23,400.00 |
|Closing Stock     $86,200.00  $81,100.00  $76,400.00  $69,100.00  $61,475.00  $95,275.00 |
|Stock Payments                                        $13,750.00  $13,750.00  $15,125.00 |
|                                                                                |
|Rent               $3,000.00                                       $3,000.00    |
|Rates etc          $2,250.00   $2,250.00   $2,250.00   $2,250.00   $2,250.00   $2,250.00 |
|Promotion          $5,000.00   $5,000.00   $5,000.00   $1,000.00   $1,000.00   $1,000.00 |
|Administration     $3,000.00   $3,000.00   $3,000.00   $3,000.00   $3,000.00   $3,000.00 |
|Salaries           $4,750.00   $4,750.00   $4,750.00   $4,750.00   $4,750.00   $4,750.00 |
|Total Expenditure $18,000.00  $15,000.00  $15,000.00  $24,750.00  $27,750.00  $26,125.00 |
|                                                                                |
|REVENUE                                                                         |
|                                                                                |
|Cash               $6,142.50   $6,597.50   $6,938.75   $7,848.75   $7,962.50   $8,190.00 |
|Credit Cards      $11,407.50  $12,252.50  $12,886.25  $14,576.25  $14,787.50  $15,210.00 |
|Total Revenue     $17,550.00  $18,850.00  $19,825.00  $22,425.00  $22,750.00  $23,400.00 |
|                                                                                |
|CASH-FLOW                                                                       |
|                                                                                |
|This mth cash-flow  ($450.00)   $3,850.00   $4,825.00  ($2,325.00) ($5,000.00) ($2,725.00)|
|Accum cash-flow     ($450.00)   $3,328.00   $8,153.00   $5,828.00     $828.00  ($1,897.00)|
|Cost of Finance       $72.00       $0.00       $0.00       $0.00       $0.00     $303.52 |
|Total Cash-flow     ($522.00)   $3,328.00   $8,153.00   $5,828.00     $828.00  ($2,200.52)|
|--------------------------------------------------------------------------------|
|                JULY       AUGUST    SEPTEMBER    OCTOBER    NOVEMBER    DECEMBER |
|--------------------------------------------------------------------------------|
|EXPENDITURE                                                                     |
|                                                                                |
|Opening Stock     $95,275.00  $96,025.00 $107,375.00  $57,600.00  $49,575.00  $45,275.00 |
|Purchases this mth $28,050.00  $41,250.00  $28,875.00  $13,750.00  $16,500.00  $16,500.00 |
|Sales this month  $27,300.00  $29,900.00  $78,650.00  $21,775.00  $20,800.00  $21,775.00 |
|Closing Stock     $96,025.00 $107,375.00  $57,600.00  $49,575.00  $45,275.00  $40,000.00 |
|Stock Payments    $15,125.00  $15,125.00  $57,200.00  $28,050.00  $41,250.00  $28,875.00 |
|                                                                                |
|Rent               $3,000.00                           $3,000.00                |
|Rates etc          $2,250.00   $2,250.00   $2,250.00   $2,250.00   $2,250.00   $2,250.00 |
|Promotion          $1,000.00   $1,000.00   $1,000.00   $1,000.00   $1,000.00   $1,000.00 |
|Administration     $3,000.00   $3,000.00   $3,000.00   $3,000.00   $3,000.00   $3,000.00 |
|Salaries           $4,750.00   $4,750.00   $4,750.00   $5,250.00   $5,250.00   $5,250.00 |
|Total Expenditure $29,125.00  $26,125.00  $68,200.00  $42,550.00  $52,750.00  $40,375.00 |
|                                                                                |
|REVENUE                                                                         |
|                                                                                |
|Cash               $9,555.00  $10,465.00  $27,527.50   $7,621.25   $7,280.00   $7,621.25 |
|Credit Cards      $17,745.00  $19,435.00  $51,122.50  $14,153.75  $13,520.00  $14,153.75 |
|Total Revenue     $27,300.00  $29,900.00  $78,650.00  $21,775.00  $20,800.00  $21,775.00 |
|                                                                                |
|CASH-FLOW                                                                       |
|                                                                                |
|This mth cash-flow ($1,825.00)  $3,775.00  $10,450.00 ($20,775.00)($31,950.00)($18,600.00)|
|Accum cash-flow   ($4,025.52)   ($894.60)   $9,412.26 ($11,362.74)($45,130.78)($70,951.70)|
|Cost of Finance      $644.08     $143.14       $0.00   $1,818.04   $7,220.92  $11,352.27 |
|Total Cash-flow   ($4,669.60) ($1,037.74)   $9,412.26 ($13,180.78)($52,351.70)($82,303.97)|
--------------------------------------------------------------------------------
```

Figure 8   Presentation example

* Commas help to make numbers easier to read. If you can find room for them you will be doing a lot to make your report more readable.
* The 'continuation' at the bottom of the page is helpful. It's always a good idea to produce a printout that can fit easily into a report. In order to do this we need to ensure that it is printed on the same width of paper as the rest of the report. That way there will be no problems with binding and with photocopying. In this example what we have done is to fit the narrative into the continuation part in the lower half of the worksheet. This is done easily using COPY FROM. The formulas need to be copied down correctly (which is not quite so easy) but the result will be a more acceptable report.

LIMITATIONS OF MULTIPLAN

Introduction

It is important to recognize that Multiplan, versatile and highly capable as it is, is not the complete answer to all our computing requirements. This is in no way to criticize it. But it would be a poor use of your time if you struggle bravely to make it do something for which it frankly was not intended. That is the reason for the inclusion of this topic in this book.

Privacy

Privacy is a common feature of large data processing systems which have large databases and many terminals. What this means, in simple terms, is an arrangement which allows only certain specified individuals access to confidential information. In microcomputers this has tended not to be an issue, and in Multiplan there are no arrangements to protect information being seen by unauthorized individuals.

Anyone who has access to Multiplan and the diskettes on which the worksheets are stored has access to all the data involved. The LOCK command protects cells and formulas against *accidental* loss. But this does not prevent your operator from looking at other parts of the worksheet, or different worksheets.

Some modified protection is possible in the following circumstances:

You have a diskette based system with only one user at a time: You only insert your data diskettes prior to using the system, you SAVE your results and remove your diskettes immediately afterwards. When not in use your data diskettes are locked away in a desk or filing cabinet.

You have a hard disk system with a multiuser capability: You order all other users away from the machine and its terminals or use the system when the building is empty. Not only do you take away your back-up diskette but you must also delete the hard disk copy of your data.

You should note that this approach prevents you being able to delegate the task of keying in the data to an operator. If the results are so confidential that only you can see them, then you will have to be your own operator. There's no way round that.

One other option remains. You make use of eXTERNAL COPY to separate the **data** from the **conclusions**. If the data is pretty harmless stuff, you can get someone to key in the data on one diskette. Then you have your analysis system on another diskette and when you have loaded it, you perform an eXTERNAL COPY from the data diskette. You keep your analysis diskette locked away and your secrets remain safe.

Large volumes

If you have an application with many thousands of transactions, think hard before you put it on Multiplan. I'm not saying it can't be done. But the likelihood gets less as the numbers get larger. What you'll have against you is the following:

* Speed: a specially designed computer system is likely to do it faster.
* Space: you'll build up significant problems of placing the data within your worksheet or worksheets.
* Validation: although the Multiplan logical functions are very suitable for validating what you key in, it's quite likely that with large volumes you'll need more complex validation with proper narrative telling the operator what the error was so that it can be rectified there and then.
* Menu driven instructions: in Multiplan the operator decides on the sequence of operation (although the 'Next Unlocked Cell' Key is certainly useful). In other systems the operator is given instructions at the screen about what to do next.

Text

There are some office tasks where you need to be able to recognize actual pieces of text. An example is testing if the name of a place is 'ROME'. Multiplan cannot do this. Be careful if you think you are going to need to do this. We have a moderately acceptable compromise to achieve this.

Suppose that in a particular column you are going to have a number of Italian cities:

Naples
Genoa
Florence
Rome
Venice

In this case I cannot enter a formula IF(CITY="ROME", ... But what I *can* do is to enter IF(LEN(CITY)=4, ... Note that this only works because the only city mentioned with four characters *is* Rome. Put Pisa in, and it doesn't work.

Cooperative worksheet development

The assumption in this book is that one person is developing a worksheet. This is often valid. But there are some occasions when a number of people are responsible for the information within the worksheet: they might be developing a new budget or some new project. It's easy enough if they all prepare their own material one at a time: they simply use the microcomputer one after the other. But suppose they are at different locations or if they want to develop their own inputs at their own terminals?

There is no difficulty if you move the diskette around: you put the basic worksheet and *your* data on a diskette and let your colleague add to it. The diskette may be carried to the next office or despatched half-way across the world: no problem.

The trouble arises if you want to use the same worksheet from different terminals. (This only becomes a realistic requirement if you have a multiuser system, with a hard disk, that supports Multiplan. They do exist and the number of them will probably increase.) In such a situation you will be able to assign read and write permissions through your operating systems. If Mr. A enters his data, SAVEs it and Ms. B enters her data and SAVEs it: no problem. But if they expect to overlap their input, so that Mr. A has not SAVEd when Ms. B LOADs: then we have a bad problem. It means that you cannot be sure of your data. It means that you need some way of ensuring that only one person is accessing that worksheet at any one time. That isn't easy, I know. But that's the only answer that's going to work.

COMMUNICATING
WITH OTHER
COMPUTER SYSTEMS

Introduction

Multiplan cannot live in isolation from what is going on around it. In business terms this means that my worksheet's results may be of interest to my colleague's payroll system. You may wish to see your worksheet reflect the results, for example, of a Sales Analysis System. Let's see if Multiplan can be of help.

TRANSFER OPTIONS

You have the TRANSFER OPTIONS sub-command to assist with this process. If we look at the Command Line when we enter it we see the following:

TRANSFER OPTIONS mode: Normal Symbolic Other   setup:

The "mode:" field is intended to enable us to communicate with other computer systems. The "setup:" is not relevant to this discussion.

Normal

The default is 'Normal' which means that we are not communicating with other systems. If we leave the mode as 'Normal' all TRANSFER LOADs and TRANSFER SAVEs will transfer the worksheets in a form that is 'natural' to Multiplan.

Symbolic

If we select 'Symbolic' then all the later SAVEs and LOADs will be in an alternative format—until we change the mode back to 'Normal'. This alternative format of the worksheets is a defined structure to which other computer systems can adapt. This structure consists of separate codes to identify cells, formulas, values, relationships such as an eXTERNAL link. (It is called SYmbolic LinK, or SYLK.) The TRANSFER time is noticeably slower as there is a lot of conversion taking place.

If you have LOADed some external data by this method you should now set the TRANSFER OPTIONS mode back to 'Normal' before you SAVE it, so that you may now use it as a standard Multiplan worksheet. If you have SAVEd a worksheet by this method a program may be written to use your data in any way that the program specification calls for.

This is a subject that requires programming expertise to use and it is covered in your manufacturer's manual. If you are not a programmer, and this book is intended primarily for people who are not, then you should seek some technical assistance in order to make the connection. The important thing to realize is that you *do* have a mechanism for two way traffic: you can get external data into Multiplan and you can get Multiplan data into an external system.

Other

The 'Other' option for the mode field is Visicalc. If you have Visicalc worksheets on your system you may 'import' them to Multiplan. That means that, having selected 'Other' in TRANSFER OPTIONS, you will be able to TRANSFER LOAD a Visicalc worksheet into your Multiplan worksheet. (You are now free to SAVE it in Multiplan format, after setting the mode back to 'Normal'.)

Note that this LOAD is a 'merge', meaning that what is loaded is added to what is already in the worksheet. If you do not wish this to happen you should TRANSFER CLEAR first. Note also that the traffic is only one way: you may not TRANSFER SAVE a Multiplan worksheet while the mode is 'Other'. The intention is obviously that you should transfer data from Visicalc to Multiplan but not in the other direction!

PRINT FILE

The other way of communicating with other systems is to PRINT to File. This means that the data that would have gone to the printer gets diverted to the diskette or hard disk instead. This can then be altered by any word processing or text processing package. This method is not recommended if you wish to do calculations on your Multiplan results. But it is a simple method of incorporating tables within a report. For more information you must consult the manual of the word processing package that you have.

PART 2
MAJOR THEMES
IN MULTIPLAN

Introduction

This part covers the major operational techniques in Multiplan, irrespective of whether they are achieved by commands, sub-commands, functions or function keys. You will be able to look to this part for the comprehensive treatment of the subjects listed below. These overlap with the treatment given in the Full Reference Guide, in Part 3. Part 2 is structured around topics, Part 3 is structured around commands and sub-commands. Where it is helpful, Part 3 refers you to Part 2: there is no need for references to Part 3 since it is self-indexing.

ACCURACY OF DATA
AND CALCULATIONS

To consider accuracy in Multiplan we must consider it from *two* points of view:

1. The **apparent** accuracy at the screen and on the printer.
2. The **real** accuracy that is inside the machine.

Apparent accuracy

We have FORMAT commands which determine the column width, the format code and the number of decimals. These things, between them, *appear* to govern the accuracy of the numbers calculated by a formula. For most purposes this is satisfactory, Multiplan will correctly handle our needs for accuracy without needing a detailed specification of what those needs are.

The general rule for displaying numbers that Multiplan observes is:

> The number will always be displayed with as many digits as can appear in the cell.

In detail the FORMAT aspects are as follows:

COLUMN WIDTH will determine how many digits *can* be displayed.

Format Code: should be considered in three parts:

> Cont (meaning Continuous) only concerns cells containing text and can be ignored.

> Exp will cause the mathematical notation to be used in displaying the number in this cell. This enables Multiplan to display both very large numbers and also very small numbers with greater accuracy.

> All the other Format Codes will display each digit for which there is room in the cell, together with the number of decimals when used.

Real accuracy

The real accuracy that Multiplan always works to is *fourteen* places of decimals. This is fine for most purposes but you may need to know about this when you are using very small numbers that are later multiplied by very large numbers. The loss of accuracy *might* be a problem.

Scientific Notation (recognized by the use of 'E') is calculated internally and stored in a range from the power of 10^{-63} to 10^{63}.

Real accuracy is modified by using the Functions which exist for this purpose:

ROUND: Which will round off the internal representation of the number of places given in parentheses.

                For example, ROUND(KWH,2) will alter the internal representation of KWH so that if it was 5.768 it now becomes 5.77, this rounded number then being used in all later calculations.

FIXED: Which will turn a number into text and limit it to a specified number of digits. This is therefore different from the 'Fix' format code of the FORMAT CELLS sub-command because that only alters the apparent accuracy of the number.

CONNECTING WORKSHEETS
TO EACH OTHER

Introduction

The ability to connect worksheets makes Multiplan a much more powerful system than its competitors. Properly understood, it is *easy* to use and *useful* in many situations. Misunderstood, as it often is, it is a barrier for many users preventing them from moving on to advanced applications of Multiplan. (This topic is often described as **linking** worksheets. In this book we call it **connecting** worksheets because linking is a special case of connecting.)

Concepts

First we'll list the concepts that we're going to introduce:

Why Connect Worksheets?
External
Supporting
Dependent
Linkage
eXTERNAL
eXTERNAL COPY
eXTERNAL LIST
eXTERNAL USE

After we've covered the concepts we'll go on to learn the Multiplan commands which are used.

Why connect worksheets?

More often than not our worksheets relate to some outside set of business circumstances. It's unrealistic to regard each operation as totally independent of the others. What we really want is to be able to relate one worksheet to another. Examples of these relationships are:

* Comparing this year's performance with other years' performance.
* Integrating one factory's production with other factories' production.
* Breaking down costs to a lower level in detailed worksheets, all contributing to the summary worksheet.

It is a matter of judgement to decide whether to implement your solution on one, possibly large, worksheet instead of several, possibly small worksheets. The advantages of splitting the job down to more worksheets are:

*   **Speed:** each smaller worksheet will run faster than one big one.

*   **Flexibility:** you're going to find it easier to make individual changes by going to the specific worksheet where the problem is.

*   **Capacity:** this way you'll be a lot safer from the danger of running out of space, when you get a '0% Free' message. Always plan on the basis of multiple worksheets, even when it looks as though you're going to have plenty of room. That way you won't get into trouble when your system grows and grows, as they sometimes do. Using multiple worksheets safeguards the future of your application.

Some new terms

In Multiplan the way you set up the connection, by eXTERNAL COPY, causes a special status to be set up. We need to accept three new terms: external, supporting and dependent.

External: any worksheet other than the one we're operating on at the moment (the active worksheet).

Supporting: after you have made the external copy, the sheet *from* which you copy is called the supporting worksheet.

Dependent: after you have made the external copy, the sheet *to* which you copy is called the dependent worksheet.

Linkage

When we copy information from a supporting to a dependent worksheet we may choose whether the copying is going to be **linked**. Linking means that every time the information in the supporting worksheet changes, this change will be reflected in the dependent worksheet when we come to review it. This is the key concept in understanding the importance of eXTERNAL COPY. It allows us to perform massive recalculations of projects and plans.

Note also that we do not *have* to link worksheets when we connect them. It's sometimes just enough to copy information from one worksheet to another. An example of this is taking last year's carry forward figures as this year's brought forward. Unless we think they are going to change there is no point in making this a linked copy. There are fewer restrictions if you make them unlinked.

eXTERNAL command

There is just one command that controls this whole process: the eXTERNAL. (It's quite often spelled this way to remind us that for the purpose of the 20 commands on the command lines it begins with the letter 'X', which is not required for anything else.) This command has three sub-commands, which enable us to perform all the actions required to control the connection of worksheets. The three sub-commands are:

* eXTERNAL COPY, which lets us copy from the supporting to the dependent worksheet, make a link if we want to, and also to unmake a link.

* eXTERNAL LIST, which lets us review at the screen· all the relationships, whether dependent or supporting, which the active worksheet has with other external worksheets.

* eXTERNAL USE, which lets us substitute one filename for another in the relationships which have previously been set up using eXTERNAL COPY.

Those are all the concepts that we need to grasp. We'll now consider in detail just how to make these connections work correctly.

THE NORMAL CASE

Introduction

We are now ready to deal with the three sub-commands of the eXTERNAL command. There is a lot of material to cover. In order to help assimilate this new material we will first consider only the normal case. This is already very powerful and the sort of thing you'll be wanting to do. We then go on to deal with the more advanced uses of eXTERNAL COPY.

How to do it

We start with the eXTERNAL COPY sub-command:

XTERNAL COPY from sheet: ▓▓▓▓ name: ▓▓▓▓ to: ▓▓▓▓ linked: Yes No

Having entered eXTERNAL COPY all you have to do is to fill in the four fields:

from sheet: You enter here the name of the external sheet that is going to become the supporting sheet. (You do not state what is to be the dependent sheet: that has to be the active sheet.)

name: You enter here the reference of the cell, or group of cells, in the external sheet that you want copied into the active sheet.

to: You enter here the cell, or group of cells to which the copy takes place. You will usually be prompted by the active cell. It's convenient to point the Cell Pointer before entering eXTERNAL COPY. But you can change the response if you want to.

linked: You choose here whether you want there to be a linkage. The proposed response is 'Yes' but you can change it. Linking means that if there is a change in the linked field in the supporting worksheet, provided you have SAVEd the supporting worksheet, then that change will show in the dependent worksheet.

Altering the connection

The next sub-command we'll look at is eXTERNAL USE. This permits us to substitute another supporting worksheet in place of the one that was used when performing an eXTERNAL COPY to the active worksheet. The name of the active worksheet doesn't get mentioned because it's not needed. We should remember that eXTERNAL USE always assumes that the dependent worksheet is the active worksheet: it's the supporting worksheet that gets changed.

It looks like this:

eXTERNAL USE filename: ▨▨▨   instead of: ▨▨▨

The 'filename:' field is prompting you to indicate the name of the **substitute** filename. The 'instead of:' field is prompting you for the worksheet that is to be substituted. There will be no proposed response for the 'filename:' and there will only be a proposed response for 'instead of:' if there has been a previous eXTERNAL USE in this worksheet during this session—in which case it will be the same as before.

Why USE it?

Why should we want to do this? A good example is when we want to produce a plan based on different assumptions—a best case, a worst case and a 'normal' case. We might set up the plan in the dependent worksheet and have three alternative supporting worksheets. We set up the eXTERNAL COPY with NORMAL as the supporting worksheet. We can switch all the connections between NORMAL and the active worksheet (there could be several eXTERNAL COPYs) to another supporting worksheet, called BEST. This saves us unmaking and remaking all the connections. We could also make another eXTERNAL USE to change it all over again to another supporting worksheet, called WORST. The structures of all the sheets involved, COPY and USE should all be the same.

Some people set up the original eXTERNAL COPY from a fictitious worksheet, just so that they can substitute other, real, worksheets in its place using eXTERNAL USE. The benefit of doing all this is speed of operation: the less you key in the more you can make use of the results.

Reviewing the connections

We use the eXTERNAL LIST sub-command to review what linkages have been made for the active worksheet. No response is required. The result is that your view of the screen changes. All the rows and columns disappear, and are replaced by the following type of information:

Sheets supporting b

a

Sheets depending on b

c

Note that you can have a long chain of relationships. What is a supporting worksheet to this one can itself be a dependent worksheet with a supporting worksheet of its own. The chain can be long. (The chain need not be only in one direction. It is possible to have 'a' depending on 'b' and 'b' depending on 'a'.)

The list takes account of substitutions which have arisen because of eXTERNAL USE. An example of this is:

Sheets supporting a

c   instead of b

When you have finished reviewing your linkages you may regain the previous screen by pressing any key.

A worked example

Having set out the main rules governing the use of the eXTERNAL COPY sub-command we'll now consider an example of its use.

We'll assume that our dependent worksheet is a summary sheet called SUMM84 looking like this:

		1	2	3	4	5	6
1	SUMM84		SNODGRASS ENTERPRISES INC				
2	– –						
3			JAN	FEB	MAR	APR	MAY
4	– –						
5	TURNOVER						
6							
7	Red						
8	Orange						
9	Yellow						
10	Green						
11	Blue						
12	Indigo						
13	Violet						
14	– – – – –						
15	TOTALS						
16	– – – – –						

(The narrative in R1C1 is a useful way of identifying worksheets that look similar.)

We'll also assume detailed Turnover worksheets for each of the months. We'll look at just one, for January, called JANU84.

	1	2	3	4	5	6
1	JANU84		SNODGRASS ENTERPRISES INC			
2	– –					
3		NORTH	SOUTH	EAST	WEST	TOTAL
4	– –					
5	TURNOVER					
6						
7	Red	12	24	36	48	120
8	Orange	11	22	33	44	110
9	Yellow	10	20	30	40	100
10	Green	9	18	27	36	90
11	Blue	8	16	24	32	80
12	Indigo	7	14	21	28	70
13	Violet	6	12	18	24	60
14	– –					
15	TOTALS	63	126	189	252	630
16	– –					

As far as the summary in SUMM84 is concerned the only figures we're going to want to look at are those in the Column headed TOTAL, that is Column 6. So we NAME R7:16C6 as TOTAL by

place the Cell Pointer to R3C6,

enter NAME,

press 'tab', thus accepting 'TOTAL' as the name,

do NOT accept R3C6 as the reference, but . . .

point to R7C6,

press colon,

point to R16C6,

press 'Return'.

You must now SAVE JANU84. Then LOAD SUMM84 and move the Cell Pointer to R7C2. What you now do is:

eXTERNAL COPY from sheet: JANU84 name: TOTAL to: R7C2
linked (Yes) No

As a result of this the dependent worksheet, SUMM84, will look like this:

		1	2	3	4	5	6
1	SUMM84		SNODGRASS ENTERPRISES INC				
2	— —						
3		JAN	FEB	MAR	APR	MAY	
4	— —						
5	TURNOVER						
6							
7	Red	120					
8	Orange	110					
9	Yellow	100					
10	Green	90					
11	Blue	80					
12	Indigo	70					
13	Violet	60					
14	— — — — — — — — —						
15	TOTALS	630					
16	— — — — — — — — —						

It should now be clear why we left out the line of dashes in SUMM84 before we made the external copy. If the dashes had been there, we would have got a 'Cannot copy into non-blank cell' message. This way we build up the line of dashes as we COPY the different months into the summary statement. Note also that we must make the formats in the receiving cells to what we want them to be: eXTERNAL COPY, unlike the normal COPY, does not copy over the formats of the sending cells.

We can now enter eXTERNAL LIST. If we do so while SUMM84 is the active worksheet we will see the following on the screen:

Sheets supporting SUMM84

JANU84

No sheets depend on SUMM84

If we enter eXTERNAL LIST from JANU84 we will see:

No sheets support JANU84

Sheets depending on JANU84

SUMM84

We may now illustrate the eXTERNAL USE sub-command. Suppose that an alternative worksheet to JANU84 had been created called JABEST. It could look like this:

	1	2	3	4	5	6
1	JABEST		SNODGRASS ENTERPRISES INC			
2	— —					
3		NORTH	SOUTH	EAST	WEST	TOTAL
4	— —					
5	TURNOVER					
6						
7	Red	120	240	360	480	1200
8	Orange	110	220	330	440	1100
9	Yellow	100	200	300	400	1000
10	Green	90	180	270	360	900
11	Blue	80	160	240	320	800
12	Indigo	70	140	210	280	700
13	Violet	60	120	180	240	600
14	— —					
15	TOTALS	630	1260	1890	2520	6300
16	— —					

If we now LOAD SUMM84 and enter

eXTERNAL USE filename: JABEST instead of: JANU84

then we will see a new table in SUMM84:

	1	2	3	4	5	6
1	SUMM84		SNODGRASS ENTERPRISES INC			
2	— —					
3		JAN	FEB	MAR	APR	MAY
4	— —					
5	TURNOVER					
6						
7	Red	1200				
8	Orange	1100				
9	Yellow	1000				
10	Green	900				
11	Blue	800				
12	Indigo	700				
13	Violet	600				
14	— — — — — — — —					
15	TOTALS	6300				
16	— — — — — — — —					

And if we enter eXTERNAL LIST in SUMM84 we will see:

Sheets supporting SUMM84

JABEST instead JANU84

No sheets depend on SUMM84

FURTHER INFORMATION

Introduction

We've now covered the basic ground of the use of multiple worksheets. Next we'll be looking at some extra refinements in the use of eXTERNAL COPY. These extra refinements are all valuable, and you'll probably get benefit from using them.

More on the eXTERNAL COPY parameters

Extra information is now presented (in addition to what was originally stated) on the use of the parameters in eXTERNAL COPY.

The "From Sheet:" parameter

You will be prompted by the name of the last external sheet used if there have been other linked eXTERNAL COPYs in this session: otherwise there will be no prompt.

The "Name:" parameter

If you use the direction key you can obtain prompts for the names that have been created by the NAME command in the worksheet you are copying from—if it has previously been linked. Although the prompt is for "name:" you may also use an Absolute Reference instead. Names are a much better idea: absolute references are *not* recalculated if the supporting sheet is changed.

The "To:" parameter

It is preferable, because less error-prone, to make the "to:" field just one cell which determines the receiving area by the 'shape' of the sending area. You will usually be prompted by the active cell, except when the "name:" field was selected by the direction key in which case you will be prompted by the reference of the name that was selected.

The "Linked:" parameter

You should only choose 'Yes' if you really need to because unlinked connections are much more flexible than linked ones.

Direction of linking

The chain need not be all in one direction. It is possible to have worksheet named 'a' depending on 'b' and 'b' depending on 'a'. It wouldn't be a likely thing you'd want to do: but it *is* possible.

eXTERNAL COPY used internally

We can make use of the eXTERNAL COPY capability in an unusual way. There is the problem of wanting to COPY the values and not the formulas. That is exactly what eXTERNAL COPY does. It works not only when copying from one worksheet to another, it also works in the case of the active worksheet provided that you use eXTERNAL COPY and not COPY. Multiplan permits the use of eXTERNAL COPY from and to the active worksheet: but remember that the copying will be from the last SAVE. This is a variation on the method of moving from one accounting period to the next which is discussed in the section entitled 'Common Problems and How to Overcome them' on page 28.

Identifying externally copied cells

If we look at the Edit Line when pointing to a cell that has been externally copied we may see immediately where it has come from. An example of this is:

[JANU84 TOTAL]

Note that it always appears in [ ] brackets. The name of the supporting worksheet comes first; then there is a space followed by the name of the copied area. This description in brackets appears like a formula. But you should not confuse it with a formula—it is different. What it refers to is just a value, or a piece of text, you use just like any other value or piece of text. eXTERNAL COPY always leaves the actual formula behind when it does its work. The information in the brackets serves to let us know the origin of the information. This happens with all eXTERNAL COPYs, whether linked or unlinked.

Using the NAME command with eXTERNAL COPY

We may capture the name of the copied field for use in the dependent worksheet. When an eXTERNAL COPY has been executed you may immediately enter a NAME command. In this case the proposed response will be in the following form:

1. Name of supporting worksheet.

2. Space.

3. Name of copied field.

If you accept this proposed response, the named area will appear in the form of:

[JANU84.TOTAL]

You can use this name when constructing formulas in the dependent worksheet showing what your data means and where it comes from. Note that the period now separates the two parts: without this period it would not be a permissible name. This newly created name may be used in exactly the same way as all other names. Remember that otherwise eXTERNAL COPY does not copy the name to the destination area. It copies neither the name nor the formula nor the format, only the value. Please note that this facility is only available *immediately* after the eXTERNAL COPY. You only have the one chance.

PROBLEM AREAS

There are a number of problem areas connected with these facilities. We're going to review them one by one, and come up with good working solutions to each of them.

The COPY that doesn't!

Most people get a 'Cannot copy into non-blank cell' message the first time they try to achieve an eXTERNAL COPY. The problem is usually this: the receiving area must be completely free to take the information coming from the sending area. What you should do is to ensure that the receiving area is not only free, but also the same shape and the same formats as the sending area. One exception is supported: the column width in the dependent worksheet may be wider. This is useful when we use eXTER-NAL COPY for summarization. The easy way to ensure this uniformity is to create all the different sheets by SAVEing from a prototype.

Changing a COPYed cell

You're not going to be able to change a cell that has had a linked eXTERNAL COPY performed upon it. You will get a 'Locked Cell may not be changed' message. The reason is that it is regarded as though it *had* been locked because it comes from a supporting worksheet. If you really need to alter the entry you must go to the support-ing worksheet and change it there.

Undoing an eXTERNAL COPY

For this reason undoing an eXTERNAL COPY isn't very easy for you. You can't just blank out the receiving cells, although you might have tried! The message you get is the same 'Unlocked cells may not be changed'. The answer is not to use BLANK at all, but to go back to the eXTERNAL COPY that started the whole thing off.

XTERNAL COPY from sheet: ▨▨▨ name: ▨▨▨ to: ▨▨▨
linked: Yes No

What you do now is to repeat *almost exactly* what you did when you set up the eXTERNAL COPY. You'll enter the same "from sheet:", "name:" and "linked:" parameters. Only one difference: you make the "to:" field blank. If anything is there you must press 'Delete' to dispose of it. When you do that you are COPYing to nowhere: so there is no COPY. You have now undone the eXTERNAL COPY. That leaves you free to start again.

Keeping the COPYed data intact

Another problem is the appearance of the data after the eXTERNAL COPY has taken place. The problem is usually failure to ensure that FORMATs of the receiving cells are the same as the sending cells. Remember that you can have a wider column width in the receiving area. In all other respects it is desirable to have the receiving area looking exactly like the sending area.

My COPY doesn't work

Some common errors with external copying:

* Until you have SAVEd the worksheets that make the connection, nothing has happened yet. If the supporting worksheet has not been SAVEd, the dependent worksheet cannot take any change into account.

* If you do not SAVE any change in the dependent worksheet eXTERNAL COPY this too will be lost.

* You can only make *one* linked connection from an area in the supporting worksheet. If you make a second one, the first will disappear. To achieve the same effect, don't use eXTERNAL COPY twice. Instead use an internal COPY command the second time.

* If you SAVE your worksheets to diskette, you will have to ensure that all the worksheets connected by eXTERNAL COPY are on the same diskette. Otherwise you will get a 'Cannot read file' message.

* If you cannot find room for all the connected worksheets on the same diskette you may have to change diskettes between eXTERNAL COPYs. In this case a 'File is not a saved worksheet' message may be alerting you to the need to change diskettes.

CURRENCY
CONSIDERATIONS

Introduction

Multiplan allows money to be expressed by means of the $ format code and also the DOLLAR function. In this section we are going to cover two things: the use of this feature, and also the choices available to those people whose currency is not the Dollar.

Use of $ and the DOLLAR function

The use of $ as a format code in the FORMAT is a quick way of ensuring the following things about the *appearance* of the value:

1. The equivalent of setting the number to a fixed number of decimals, namely 2.

2. The $ sign is right up against the number, however small or large it is.

3. If the value is negative this is signified by placing the amount in parentheses. (It is in order to leave room for the right parenthesis that the rightmost position of a numeric cell is generally not occupied.)

The use of the DOLLAR function alters the value *internally* as well as externally. This creates a piece of text which has the same external characteristics as the $ response to the "format code:" field and it is left justified. The difference is that a cell that has had the DOLLAR function invoked cannot be used in calculation. However, it may be used in concatenation.

Currency which is not Dollars

If you use a currency that is not the Dollar then you should find out if you have a local version of Multiplan. We will consider what your best use of currency is in the case where you *do* have a local currency version and also the case where you do *not* have a local currency version.

If you have a local currency version of Multiplan you can simply read everything that has been said about $ and DOLLAR and replace it in your mind with your own local currency symbol. Just one problem remains: you will need to ensure that the printer recognizes your own currency symbol. If it doesn't you are not going to be satisfied with just looking at your symbol on the screen. This is a problem between your computer and your printer.

If you appear to make no progress, consider one option open to you. Using the PRINT FILE sub-command, you can write a disk version of your printfile. If you run this file through a word processing program you can replace the currency symbol produced by Multiplan (or indeed the $ sign) with another one which your printer interprets as your national currency symbol.

If you do not have a local version of Multiplan available then you can still consider one or more of the following suggestions:

1. Putting the local currency symbol as heading information at the head of the Column containing the financial information.

2. Using MID, LEN and & to replace the $ sign by your national currency symbol.

3. Using a word processing package to convert all those $ symbols into the symbols that you want.

EDITING TECHNIQUES

Introduction

Note that editing is an important productivity aid to those who set up the Multiplan worksheet. Not to master the technique is to deprive yourself of this powerful aid that is available to you.

You can edit under the following different circumstances:

* Amending a formula that has already been entered into a cell.

* Going back while entering a formula, or any other response, to a command.

* Amending a piece of text in a cell, whether it was put there as a result of an ALPHA or a COPY command.

Editing keys

The keys available are machine dependent. You can identify the keys that you need either by looking at your manufacturer's manual or by using HELP KEYBOARD, when you can see on your screen which keys you should use. You will need keys to perform the following five operations:

* Move a character to the left, highlighting the next character.

* Move a character to the right, highlighting the next character.

* Move a word to the left (word is defined in the Quick Reference Guide), highlighting the next word.

* Move a word to the right, highlighting the next word.

* Delete the character or word that is being highlighted.

* Insertion takes place by just keying in. What you key will be inserted at the position that is being highlighted.

FORMATTING

Introduction

When we talk about formatting we are referring to the ways in which Multiplan allows us to specify the appearance of our information on the screen and on the printer. We use the formatting commands in order to make the worksheets look more professional and easy to understand.

Formatting in Multiplan is both powerful and complex. To get really full value out of Multiplan you are advised to read this section carefully. The main reason for this complexity is the fact that it *is* so powerful. The power is achieved by having many different features and facilities which interact with each other. When you have mastered the full range of its complexity you will be able to be far more effective in your use of Multiplan.

We will first of all discuss the fundamental concepts involved in formatting, before dealing with the commands and sub-commands which perform the formatting.

Concepts

There are five formatting concepts that we need to establish. They are:

1. **Column Width:** any column in the worksheet can be between 3 and 32 character positions wide. A character position is the space that is occupied by a letter, a number or a symbol.

2. **Alignment:** in Multiplan we can control where the numbers and the text will appear in the cell. Alignment will decide whether the information will appear at the left, the right or the center of a cell.

3. **Format Code:** controls the way the information is shown, for example: how many decimals will appear.

4. **Commas:** controls the appearance of the comma between the thousands and the hundreds, as in 18,632. Without this formatting feature the same number would appear as 18632.

5. **Formulas:** permits you to display the **formulas** in those cells that have them, instead of their **contents** which you normally see.

Where necessary these concepts are described in greater detail later. For the moment it's better to continue with the principles of formatting.

General formats

When we start a new worksheet we are given certain formatting choices that Multiplan makes for us. There are five of these to match the five concepts that we have just looked at:

1. All column widths are set at 10 character positions.

2. All alignments are set at 'General' meaning that text is left justified and numbers are right justified.

3. All format codes are set at 'General' meaning that Multiplan seeks to display the information that was keyed in as accurately as the space allows.

4. No commas are inserted into numeric information anywhere in the worksheet.

5. Formulas are not displayed anywhere in the worksheet: what we see is the results of the formulas.

User controlled formats

Having started with these choices made for us by Multiplan we can decide our own choices which, when we make them, supersede the choices made for us. These choices are made *either* for the whole worksheet *or* for individual cells or groups of cells. To understand this it is useful to think of three **levels** of formatting.

Levels of formatting

Level 1 The choices that Multiplan made for the whole worksheet, called **General**.

Level 2 The choices that you make yourself for the whole worksheet, called **Default**.

Level 3 The choices that you make yourself for individual cells or groups of cells: these are the ordinary FORMAT commands.

We can now relate these three levels to the sub-commands that belong to the FORMAT command.

	WIDTH	ALIGNMENT and FORMAT CODE	COMMAS and FORMULAS
LEVEL 1	10	General	No commas or formulas displayed
LEVEL 2	FORMAT DEFAULT WIDTH	FORMAT DEFAULT CELLS	FORMAT OPTIONS
LEVEL 3	FORMAT WIDTH	FORMAT CELLS	None available

To summarize the position:

Level 1 is what we got when we started the worksheet.
If we're happy with these choices then we don't need to go down to levels 2 or 3.

Level 2 lets us set the following defaults for the worksheet:
FORMAT DEFAULT WIDTH sets a uniform width for all the columns.
FORMAT DEFAULT CELLS sets uniform Alignments and Format Codes for the entire worksheet.
FORMAT OPTIONS lets us specify our commas, or formulas, or both for the entire worksheet.

Level 3 allows us to set:
The width of one or more columns using FORMAT WIDTH.
The Alignment and Format Code of a cell or group of cells using the FORMAT CELLS sub-command.

Note that there is no sub-command for commas or formulas for a cell or a group of cells, because we can only set these for the entire worksheet.

Casual and advanced users

We are now going to consider how to use these facilities. We are going to distin-guish between the **casual** user of Multiplan and the **advanced** user. The difference is important because:

The **casual** user does not want to be burdened with a lot more rules than are really needed.

The **advanced** user is entitled to be shown how Multiplan can make worksheet preparation a quicker and less repetitive operation.

COLUMN WIDTH

	WIDTH	ALIGNMENT and FORMAT CODE	COMMAS and FORMULAS
LEVEL 1	10	General	No commas or formulas displayed
LEVEL 2	FORMAT DEFAULT WIDTH	FORMAT DEFAULT CELLS	FORMAT OPTIONS
LEVEL 3	FORMAT WIDTH	FORMAT CELLS	None available

The three levels

The three levels relate to column widths in this manner:

* If you specify nothing, using neither FORMAT WIDTH *nor* FORMAT DEFAULT WIDTH, then you just get every column 10 character positions wide. This suits a lot of people a lot of the time. If you do not wish to alter column widths you do not need to use FORMAT WIDTH or FORMAT DEFAULT WIDTH.

* If you only want to alter the column width of the occasional column then you need only use FORMAT WIDTH.

* You might want to use FORMAT DEFAULT WIDTH if you are an **advanced** user of Multiplan.

The advanced user

Setting column widths for the entire worksheet can make sense if you are an advanced user. The advantage of doing this is:

* If all your columns should be, say, 12 positions wide it is better to use the FORMAT DEFAULT WIDTH command because if you need to INSERT any columns they will immediately have the default width, in this case 12. This saves having to keep using FORMAT WIDTH every time you have to insert.

In short, if you have a 'tidy' mind, you may prefer to set the column widths of the whole worksheet.

Remember that you can always:

* Set the whole worksheet to a uniform width and then alter individual column widths.

* Set individual widths and *then* set a uniform width for the columns that have not had individual widths set.

How to use them

Having established the purpose of the two WIDTH sub-commands, please refer to the Full Reference Guide for information on how to use them.

FORMATTING CELLS

	WIDTH	ALIGNMENT and FORMAT CODE	COMMAS and FORMULAS
LEVEL 1	10	General	No commas or formulas displayed
LEVEL 2	FORMAT DEFAULT WIDTH	FORMAT DEFAULT CELLS	FORMAT OPTIONS
LEVEL 3	FORMAT WIDTH	FORMAT CELLS	None available

The three levels

The three levels relate to formatting in this manner:

* If you specify nothing, using neither FORMAT CELLS *nor* FORMAT DEFAULT CELLS, then you just get the General formats. This is unlikely to suit you all the time. But if you never need to alter any formats then you do not need to use FORMAT CELLS or FORMAT DEFAULT CELLS.

* To alter the alignment or the format code of an individual cell, or group of cells, you use the FORMAT CELLS command.

* You might want to use FORMAT DEFAULT CELLS if you are an **advanced** user of Multiplan.

The advanced user

Setting the alignment or the format code for the entire worksheet can make sense if you are an advanced user. The advantage of doing this is:

* If all your format codes should be, say, 'Integer' it is better to use the FORMAT DEFAULT CELLS command because as you develop your worksheet you would have to keep on issuing FORMAT CELLS commands. This way you can do it just once and save yourself time.

In short, if most of your cells require a uniform format code, say 'Int', '$' or 'Fix' with # of decimals: 2, then you can save time with FORMAT DEFAULT CELLS.
Remember that you can always:

* Set the whole worksheet to a uniform format code or alignment and then alter individual format codes and alignments.

* Set formats for individual cells and *then* set a uniform format for the cells that have not had individual formats set.

The fields for formatting cells

The two sub-commands for formatting cells have almost identical fields that need to be entered. The fields are:

* Alignment.
* Format Code.
* # of characters.

Alignment

Alignment governs where in the cell the contents will appear. The options available are:

FORMAT CELLS		Def	Ctr	Gen Left	Right	—
FORMAT DEFAULT CELLS			Ctr	Gen Left	Right	

Note that FORMAT CELLS has two more options than FORMAT DEFAULT CELLS: 'Def' and '—'. Whenever you enter either of the two cell formatting sub-commands you will see the **current** status of alignment because it is *either* highlighted if you are entering the current field, *or* in parentheses if you are entering another field.

Def   Only available in the FORMAT CELLS sub-command. It allows you to accept whatever you may have chosen for alignment in the FORMAT DEFAULT CELLS sub-command. In fact it is the initial proposed response for the FORMAT CELLS sub-command: later you will see what you last put there in this sub-command.

Ctr   Places the cell's contents as centrally as possible. Available for both sub-commands.

Gen   Left justifies text, right justifies numeric information. Available for both sub-commands. It is the initial proposed response for FORMAT DEFAULT CELLS.

Left   Left justifies all information. Available for both sub-commands.

Right   Right justifies all information. Available for both sub-commands.

—   Allows you to leave the alignment unchanged from what it was before. Available for FORMAT CELLS only. You would use it if you were using FORMAT CELLS and altering the format codes of a group of cells in a uniform way and wanted to leave the Alignment unchanged in the different cells within the group of cells.

Format code

Format Codes enable us to specify the way the cell's contents appear. The options available are:

FORMAT CELLS   Def Cont Exp Fix Gen Int $ * % −

FORMAT DEFAULT CELLS   Cont Exp Fix Gen Int $ * %

Note that FORMAT CELLS has two more options than FORMAT DEFAULT CELLS: 'Def' and '−'. Whenever you enter either of the two cell formatting sub-commands you will see the **current** format code because it is *either* highlighted if you are entering the format code, *or* in parentheses if you are entering another field.

Def   Allows you to choose the default that was set up with the FORMAT DEFAULT CELLS sub-command (if there was one) in the FORMAT CELLS sub-command. It is the initial proposed response for FORMAT CELLS. Later you will see what you last put there in this sub-command.

Cont Applies only to cells containing text. You give adjacent cells in the same row this format code so that the text can continue without stopping at the first cell's boundaries. You would use it for the heading of a worksheet which goes across several columns. Available for both sub-commands.

Exp   Specifies mathematical notation. Used to hold large and small numbers within the cell. Available for both sub-commands. Examples are:

Number	*Exponential*
0.0023	23E−04
12.000	12E
3,000,000	3E+06

Fix   Specifies a **fixed** number of decimals in the number. You will have to respond to the "# of decimals" field to indicate how many. Where there is rounding it goes up: 2.785 becomes 2.79. Available for both sub-commands.

Gen   Retains the 'General' default for format codes:

      Numbers are expressed in the form that they were entered, and if there is not room for all the digits then mathematical notation is used.

      Text is displayed with whatever alignment has been chosen and with as many characters as there is room for.

      The results of formulas are displayed with the minimum number of digits needed—for instance, 3.00*2.40 becomes 7.2.

      Available for both sub-commands.

Int   Ensures that the numeric information is displayed in **integer** form, that is the decimal part is ignored for the purpose of display. Where there is rounding it goes up: 98.5 becomes 99. Available for both sub-commands.

$ Ensures that the numeric information is displayed in the form of a money amount with:

> $ sign before the first digit, however large or small the number is.

> Two decimals, meaning cents, without having to specify them in the "# of decimals" field.

> Parentheses around the amount if it is negative (it is in order to leave room for the right parenthesis that the rightmost position of a numeric cell is generally not occupied).

*   Ensures that numeric information is displayed in the form of a bar-chart.

%   Ensures that the numeric information is displayed in the form of percentages.

−   Allows you to leave the format code unchanged from what it was before. Available for FORMAT CELLS only. You would use it if you were using FORMAT CELLS and you were altering the alignment codes of a group of cells in a uniform way and wanted to leave the Format unchanged in the different cells within the group of cells.

of decimals

of decimals   Required if the 'Fix', 'Exp' or '%' option was chosen for the format codes. You specify the number of decimals that the specified cells have. A few examples are given:

> If the 'fix' specifies three decimals:

Before	After
35	35.000
25.8963	25.896
1000.258	1000.258

Note that you *only* need to make responses to the "# of decimals" field if you have chosen the 'Fix', 'Exp' or '%' response to the "format code:" field. In particular $ does not require a response because a response of 2 is implied. In those cases where '# of decimals' does not apply you may skip past the field by pressing 'Return'. Whatever is proposed, or entered, in that field is ignored if it does not apply.

FORMAT OPTIONS

	WIDTH	ALIGNMENT and FORMAT CODE	COMMAS and FORMULAS
LEVEL 1	10	General	No commas or formulas displayed
LEVEL 2	FORMAT DEFAULT WIDTH	FORMAT DEFAULT CELLS	FORMAT OPTIONS
LEVEL 3	FORMAT WIDTH	FORMAT CELLS	None available

The last of the five FORMAT sub-commands is FORMAT OPTIONS.

FORMAT OPTIONS commas: Yes No   formulas: Yes No

There are two fields that have a yes/no setting. They are "commas:" and "formulas:".

Commas

The ability to enter commas into a worksheet is very useful when we want to improve the presentation of our material. It is much easier to read '34,730,216' than '34730216'. Note two things about the commas option:

* It applies to the whole worksheet.

* Only the numbers with a Format Code of Int, Fix, $ and % will be displayed with the commas. Other numbers will not be displayed with a comma.

The first point could be inconvenient when you have the year entered in a cell. The year expressed as 1,984 is not acceptable. The answer to this problem is to take advantage of the second point: express year as 'Gen' and the problem is solved.

Formulas

Choosing to display formulas has the effect of replacing the display of the results of formulas by the display of the formulas themselves, in the cells that have formulas. Other cells continue to display text or numbers.

You would use this choice when you are troubleshooting. When the worksheet behaves in a way that you don't expect, you can use FORMAT OPTIONS formulas: 'Yes', to reveal what formulas you *have* got as opposed to the formulas as you *think* you've got. Then, when you have corrected the mistake, you change the "formulas" setting back to 'No'.

FUNCTIONS IN GENERAL

Introduction

Of the 42 Functions available in Multiplan, many are so specialized that they do not require treatment in this book. If you want to know how to use them you won't need this book to tell you. Examples of this point can be found in functions such as TAN, PI, LN and EXP. These are not covered in this section. Other functions fall naturally into other topics, such as LEN or DELTA. As they are covered in the sections on 'Text Functions' and 'Iteration', they are therefore not covered here. The purpose of this section is to cover the remaining functions which do not get covered elsewhere, yet merit treatment in this book.

LOOKUP

Consider this table:

	1	2	3
1			
2		QUANTITY	DISCOUNT
3		— — — — —	— — — — —
4		1	0
5		10	5
6		30	10
7		50	20
8		100	35
9		200	45
10			
11		Quantity	
12		Discount	

This is an example of a discount structure, where if greater quantities are ordered, larger discounts are available. If you place, say, 19 in R11C3 you can then test it out. In R12C3 you must enter:

1   = to enter a function
2   LOOKUP
3   (
4   point to R11C3, giving you R[-1]C
5   ,
6   point to R4C2, giving you R[-8]C[-1]
7   :
8   point to R9C3, giving you R[-3]C
9   )

The whole entry will be: LOOKUP(R[-1]C,R[-8]C[-1]:R[-3]C). The result will be 5. You may also use a name for the area occupied by the table and for the quantity.

11   Quantity   19
12   Discount   5

As you change the entry for 'Quantity', so the result for 'Discount' also changes. You should appreciate that the LOOKUP process takes note of the 'shape' of the lookup table. This example shows a table that is taller than it is wide: therefore the left column is used for looking up and the right column is used for extracting the results.

Consider the case of a table that is wider than it is tall:

	1	2	3	4	5	6
1						
2	QUANTITY	1	10	30	50	100
3	DISCOUNT	0	5	10	20	35

In this case the LOOKUP will use the first row for looking up and the second row for extracting the results.

INDEX

We may use a more elaborate structure in which we look up both horizontally and vertically. In Multiplan this is called an Index. Consider this table which shows us the distance from any depot to any shop.

	1	2	3	4	5	6
1			Depots			
2						
3	Shops		1	2	3	4
4						
5	Abdulla	1	405	488	330	226
6	Bulango	2	160	176	248	451
7	Cohen	3	52	56	128	341
8	Drucker	4	86	188	73	279
9	Ewart	5	43	106	58	270
10						
11	Shop:		Depot:		Distance:	
12						

In this case no use is made of the shape since the lookup is both horizontal and vertical. If you enter a shop number, say 4, in R11C2 and a depot number, say 2, in R11C4 then you can extract the distance, in this case 188, by entering in R11C6 the formula:

```
 1  INDEX
 2  (
 3  point to the 405 in R5C3, giving you R[-6]C[-3]
 4  :
 5  point to the 270 in R9C6, giving you R[-2]C
 6  ,
 7  point to the 4 in R11C2, giving you RC[-4]
 8  ,
 9  point to the 2 in RR11C4, giving you RC[-2]
10  )
```

The whole entry will be

INDEX(R[-6]C[-3]:R[-2]C,RC[-4],RC[-2])

You may use a name for all the references used. The answer will be:

10	— —					
11	Shop:	4	Depot:	2	Distance:	188
12	— —					

MOD

Another function is available which lets us find out the remainder after a division operation. This is called MOD, which stands for Modulo.

If I have a value in a cell and want to know the remainder after I have divided it by 6: this is what I must do. I put the value in a cell named, say, 'Total'. I then place the Cell Pointer elsewhere and enter MOD(Total,6). If 'Total' contains 13, then the answer to the formula will be 1.

NPV

Net Present Value is a commonly used commercial concept. It enables us to calculate the amount of cash I must find *now* to produce income in the future. The most obvious use is in decisions concerning investment. Here is an example:

	1	2	3	4	5	6	7
1	PURCHASE	$14,500.00					
2							
3	LEASE						
4	YEAR 1	$4,000,00					
5	YEAR 2	$4,000.00					
6	YEAR 3	$4,000.00					
7	YEAR 4	$4,000.00					
8	YEAR 5	$4,000.00					
9							
10	TOTAL	$20,000.00					
11							
12	RATE		0.06	0.08	0.10	0.12	0.14
13							
14	NPV						
15							
16	ACTION						

Note that the rates in Row 12 refer to interest rates. Multiplan is not going to tell you what these are going to be for a five-year period: you will have to make your own assessment of what the interest rates might be. Note also that the interest rates, which we refer to as '10%', etc., must appear as decimals.

Next you should enter in R14C2:

1   = to introduce the function
2   NPV
3   (
4   point to the 0.06 in R12C2, giving you R[−2]C
5   ,
6   point to the first $4,000 in R4C2, *and* press the 'Reference' Function Key
     making this an Absolute Reference
7   :
8   point to the last $4,000 in R8C2, *and* press 'Reference'
9   )

The full entry is NPV(R[−2]C,R4C2:R8C2).

Now we'll put something in R16C2:

1   = to introduce the function
2   IF
3   (
4   point to the $16,849.46 now in R14C2, giving you R[−2]C
5   <
6   point to the $14,500.00 in R1C2, *and* press 'Reference' making this an
     Absolute Reference
7   ,
8   point to the word "LEASE" in R3C1 and press 'Reference'
9   ,
10   point to the word "PURCHASE" in R1C1 and press 'Reference'
11   )

The full entry is IF(R[−2]C<R1C2,R3C1,R1C1).

This is going to advise you whether it's better to purchase or lease. Note also that the references to the words "PURCHASE" and "LEASE" must be absolute references. You can now COPY RIGHT from R14C2 and R16C2 by four places.
The result will be:

12	RATE	0.06	0.08	0.10	0.12	0.14
13						
14	NPV	$16,849.46	$15,970.84	$15,163.15	$14,419.10	$13,732.32
15						
16	ACTION	PURCHASE	PURCHASE	PURCHASE	LEASE	LEASE

As you see this is a useful mechanism: it enables you to make strategic decisions for leasing and purchasing at different interest rates.

ITERATION

Introduction

Iteration is very much a minority interest among Multiplan users. It is very powerful and very relevant in certain situations. It is also not needed by most people who use Multiplan. You are advised not to get into this subject unless you really need it.

What is it?

The easiest way to explain what iteration means is to look at an example. Consider the following cash flow forecast:

	January	February	March
Opening Balance	$1,000.00		
Receipts	$10,000.00		
Payments	$12,000.00		
Interest			
Closing Balance			

We will also imagine that we need to know two more things:

1. The Closing Balance, for which we need to know the Interest Charge.

2. The Interest Charge, for which we need to know the Closing Balance.

Multiplan is able to help us with this problem by the process of iteration. This means that each is calculated by a formula which includes the other, and this process continues until either Multiplan or you decide to stop. If this is of no interest to you: don't worry, Multiplan has many other interesting features.

How to do it

Assuming an annual interest rate of 10 per cent (which is divided by 12 to give a monthly rate) on negative closing balances this what we do:

1. For the January Interest figure we enter

    IF(R[+1]C<0,R[+1]C*10%/12,0)

    remembering that we point to the cell underneath to obtain the R[+1]C.

2. For the Closing Balance we enter (using the pointing method):

    R[-4]C+R[-3]C-R[-2]C-R[-1]C

The immediate result is to get the computer 'beeping' at us, and we will get a message on the Message Line saying 'Circular References Unresolved'. This is because most times when such a thing is entered it is by mistake.

But this time it's no mistake: we really do want the computer to come up with an answer that satisfies both of these apparently conflicting needs. You must enter the OPTIONS command. The third field in that command allows you to specify a 'Yes' or 'No' response against the "iteration:" prompt. The default is 'No'. This is the occasion when we choose 'Yes'. If you do this you will see the two cells changing their values continually until they come to rest. When they stop we know that iteration has ended.

When they come to rest the screen will appear like this.

	January	February	March
Opening Balance	$1,000.00		
Receipts	$10,000.00		
Payments	$12,000.00		
Interest	($8.26)		
Closing Balance	($991.74)		

Note that the formula for the Interest amount needs the IF test, because interest is only charged on negative amounts. We can extend this cash flow statement to include February and March. The February Opening Balance Formula will just point to the January Closing Balance. This can be COPYed Right 1 place. Interest and Closing Balance can be COPYed Right 2 places. We may enter our own figures for Receipts and Payments in February and March. The result could look like this:

	January	February	March
Opening Balance	$1,000.00	($991.74)	$8.26
Receipts	$10,000.00	$11,000.00	$10,000.00
Payments	$12,000.00	$10,000.00	$12,000.00
Interest	($8.26)	$0.00	($16.46)
Closing Balance	($991.74)	$8.26	($1,975.27)

DELTA( )

The calculation of the Interest Payment in this example takes place quite quickly. This is because the values are close to convergence. Convergence is a mathematical term meaning that the numbers are getting closer to an acceptable solution. Under normal circumstances such as the example we have just worked through, the process of iteration comes to an end as soon as the difference in the cells being calculated is no greater than 0.001. This will suit us: it is to the nearest penny.

You may observe this process at work. If you enter DELTA( ) two cells below the Closing Balance in January you will see the differences being displayed. You can restart the process of calculation by changing one of the values that go toward the calculation. You can also press the 'Recalculate' key (F4 on the IBM PC). Remember that this is not *doing* anything to the calculation: it allows you to watch it.

Completion Test at

You may specify a completion test telling Multiplan when to stop the process of iteration. Note that you do not *have* to do this: the value of 0.001 is assumed and can be observed in DELTA( ). But you may choose another completion test which you may place in a specific cell. This test may take the form of RC[−2]>RC[−1] which simply means that as soon as the condition specified becomes true, then iteration comes to an end. You indicate the completion test in the fourth field in the OPTIONS command: you enter the reference (or the name) of the Cell that contains the condition for terminating the process of iteration. You may use the arrow keys to point to the cell that contains the condition. You can then observe during the iteration process the cell containing the condition: it displays 'FALSE' until the condition is satisfied. Then it displays 'TRUE' and iteration comes to an end.

ITERCNT( )

Also associated with iteration is the ITERCNT( ) (meaning iteration count) function. This counts the number of times a calculation has been repeated before termination is reached. This is generally of interest to statisticians, but has a special use which is of general interest.

A cell may normally only contain *either* a value *or* a formula. Sometimes you may want to start off with a value and then use a formula instead. Before iteration commences the value of ITERCNT( ) is not zero, but has the internal value of NA( ). Therefore we can use the ISNA( ) function. We could enter the following:

IF(ISNA(ITERCNT( )), 100000,R[−2]C)

This means that the current cell will contain 10,000 at the start of iteration and the contents of the cell two rows up at all other times.

Conclusion

Iteration is a big subject on its own. If you wish to pursue this you are advised to start with some simple models and experiment with them before building up more ambitious examples.

LOGICAL OPERATIONS

Introduction

'Logical Operations' is a term used in this book to refer to a number of the Functions which exist in Multiplan. This is the whole list of these functions:

    IF
    AND   OR   NOT
    TRUE   FALSE
    ISERROR
    NA   ISNA

The list given here groups these logical functions in sets which are best explained together.

If you are a **casual user** of Multiplan you are likely (though not even certain) to need only IF. So you are advised to master IF and then omit the remaining logical functions. **Advanced users** are likely to obtain benefit from studying all the logical functions.

IF

The ability to choose between two courses of action depending on the result of previous calculations is one of the most important definitions of a computer as opposed to a calculator. Worksheets become much more powerful when we can make these choices depend on the result of calculations in the worksheet itself.

The structure of the IF function is simple to understand and easy to use. It works like this:

    IF(condition,action 1,action 2)

This means that if the condition is true then the computer will perform action 1. Otherwise action 2 will be performed. This is now illustrated:

    IF(Stock<Minimum,"Re-order"," ")

This causes the computer to display the word "Re-order" if the Stock Amount (which may vary daily) has fallen below a re-order level.

Please note the following points of explanation:

* This structure of parentheses and commas is essential in all its details. Omitting even just *one* of them causes an 'Error in formula' Error Message to occur. If there is an error you may edit it.

* The parentheses must enclose all the elements in the IF function.

* In this example our condition is 'Stock<Minimum', which is either true or it is not. (We may assume that the correct cells have been given these names to make the example more readable.) The < symbol means 'less than'. It is known as a logical operator.

* The commas separate the three elements in the IF function: the condition and the two actions.

Uses

You may now consider some examples which show you how valuable this logical function is.

Exception Reporting

The stock re-ordering example is an instance of exception reporting where we make use of the choice capability to point out things that need attention. This is much better than making people search through pages of printout to look for a condition to which the computer can alert them.

Conditional Display

You can also use IF to display all the debit items in one column and all the credit items in another.

Complex Conditions

The advanced user will use IF in complex conditions where several functions are nested together.

Warning

You should be aware of the fact that the condition *must* relate to numeric information. But there is another way to get there. If you want to perform conditional display so that only Head Office costs appear in a column, then you cannot use a condition that reads R13C1="Head Office". What you can do is to give Head Office a number (as well as a name if you want to print the name). The number can then appear in a condition.

IF(R13C1=11,costs," ")

OR, AND, NOT

We often find that a condition needs to be more elaborate than it was in the example considered with the IF function. For example, we need to display costs if R13C1 is *either* 11 *or* 21. For this we have the separate OR function.

The previous example would therefore be extended to:

IF(OR(R13C1=11,R13C1=21),costs,0)

This structure is not the same as in the English language but conforms to the rule applying to all functions that the Function appears *first*, and is then followed by the parameters (called **arguments** in your manufacturer's manual).

Please note the following important points about OR.

*   OR's structure is to place a list within parentheses. You can go on adding items to the list provided you separate the items in the list with a comma and you enclose the entire list within parentheses.

*   What OR really means is that all the items in the list are examined to see if *any* of them are true.

*   What then happens is not controlled by OR itself. In this example costs are displayed if *either* condition is true, and it is the IF function which does the work.

The same structure is used by the AND function, though the meaning is importantly different. One example should be sufficient:

IF(AND(Consumption<100,Heat_loss<5),"GOOD"," ")

The new feature introduced to the explanation is:

*   AND means that the items in the list are examined to see if *all* of them are true. In the example the word "GOOD" is only displayed if both of the two conditions are true. Please note that you are not restricted to two conditions.

We may also consider the NOT function. This merely reverses the logic of what would otherwise happen.

IF(NOT(Stock>Minimum)," ","Re-Order")

This appears to be the exact opposite of the example of the simple IF command but has the same effect. If stock is NOT greater than the minimum then it is less.

This example is fairly indicative of the relevance of NOT in most situations but you can usually achieve the same effect by another method. And that other method is usually easier to understand. Therefore, the advice given here is to ignore the NOT function.

TRUE( ), FALSE( )

Two more logical functions take us further in the direction of achieving complex logic.

We need now to establish a new concept. This is that TRUE and FALSE are attributes of a cell that can be tested elsewhere.

For instance, if R30C20 contains a formula with a condition in it, that condition is either true or false. This will always be correct, irrespective of what that condition is. What we are now going to consider is a method of testing that truthfulness or falseness. So if in R31C20 we enter

IF(R30C20=TRUE( ),"YES","NO")

we will be able to print selectively according to whether the condition is correct or not. Please note:

* The parentheses after the two functions *are* necessary to Multiplan although they achieve no obvious purpose. They are there to distinguish these functions from user defined names.

* TRUE( ) and FALSE( ) are natural opposites just like IF and IF NOT.

* You can also assign a numerical value to TRUE( ) and FALSE( ). The values are 1 and 0 respectively. You could therefore test

IF(R30C20=1,"YES","NO")

This would have the same effect as the previous test for TRUE( ). The value of this is limited:

You save a few keystrokes, but the readability of the worksheet suffers.
You can also use these values in a calculation: a smart thing to do only if you can guarantee no readability problems.

* You can even leave out any explicit reference to the TRUE condition:

IF(R30C20,"YES","NO")

This saves even more key strokes but does greatest damage to readability. But you can use it if you want to . . . .

ISERROR

When we use computers we must always plan for error conditions. A number of error states are notified by Multiplan:

#DIV/0
#NAME?
#NULL!
#NUM!
#N/A
#REF
#VALUE

What ISERROR allows us to do is to check for the existence of one of these errors. They can be thought of as being TRUE and FALSE: a cell either has or does not have an error condition.

This is a useful function for the advanced Multiplan user because it can detect an error and prevent it being displayed as an error.

IF(ISERROR(Wages/Hours),'' '',Wages/Hours)

You can build up some quite complex logic using the ISERROR function.

NA, ISNA

NA is of value outside of logical operations. The obvious use is when you have a column of figures with some entries incomplete: you don't yet have the information. Putting zero in those cells can be misleading because zero is itself an entry. So you can enter NA( ) meaning that the information is not available at present. (The parentheses are there to let Multiplan recognize the function and not get confused with any Names you may have used.) What you see on the screen and in the printout is #NA—*not* NA( ).

Any formulas that use the cell with an NA in it will produce an answer of NA. This is usually exactly what you want because it is warning you that your information is incomplete. The remedy is to enter the missing item!

Life is not always as simple as that. The advanced user may consider **testing** for this. A simple example lets us perform conditional display of the sort that was introduced when we considered IF. For instance:

IF(ISNA(Total),''Data Incomplete'',Total)

(We are assuming that 'Total' is a name that you have given to a cell with total values which *may* have an NA in them.)

LOOKING AFTER MEMORY

Introduction

Running out of space is a common problem with computer systems and tends to be highly inconvenient when it happens. It is always wise to be on your guard against this. Having said that, I think that it is unlikely to cause you a problem in your use of Multiplan, particularly if you take the advice contained in this book.

Memory indicator

You can always see exactly how your use of memory is going along. On the bottom line of your screen, the Status Line, shows towards the right a " % Free" indicator. This warns if you're getting into trouble.

What uses memory up

As the cells get filled the 'Memory Free' goes down. You're not going to be able to spot a direct relationship between the number of cells being used up and the percentage of memory disappearing. It's not as simple as that.

The percentage depends mainly on two factors:

* The contents of the cells that are used.

* The 'shape' of the worksheet at the moment.

The amount of information in a cell varies. This means that a number of very full cells will take up more space than a smaller number of emptier cells.

In deciding how big your worksheet is Multiplan will take into account the smallest rectangle that includes all the cells that have been used. Consider Figure 9, which shows a worksheet where space has been allocated in a wasteful fashion. By rearranging your cells you could make the rectangle smaller. Remember that FORMATs also count towards the rectangle.

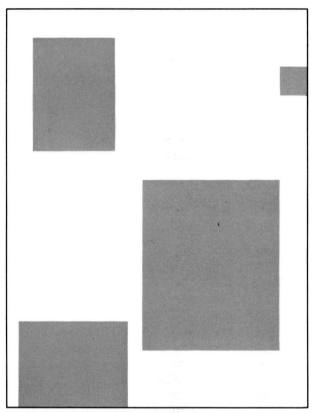

Figure 9   Example of the wasteful use of space in a worksheet. The large rectangle's shape is determined by the
position of the four smaller rectangles

Avoiding the problem

But you should not really have to count the number of cells you need. The reason is that long before your worksheet becomes so large that its size may be critical you should be thinking if you need to use the eXTERNAL command. There are many advantages and no real disadvantages in splitting your work up over several work- sheets. Most big worksheets involve repeating rather similar information over and over. Think seriously about splitting the work up. Linking is really easy once you have grasped the method.

Space and time

Another reason for being interested in the space being used up is that more space means more time. Every time you key in something Multiplan will evaluate all the formulas. This takes longer as the worksheet gets bigger. (But remember that you can switch recalculation off using the first field in the Options command.) You will see the effect of the large worksheet because as it gets larger and recalculation takes place, the 'Cells to recalculate' figure gets larger; as it gets larger you have to wait longer.

Running out

If, nevertheless, you do run out of space the following will happen.

First you will see the " % Free" Indicator becoming very small. As soon as it reaches 1% you should start being careful. When it reaches 0% you have to take notice! But Multiplan still gives you a chance. You can still use a few more commands. TRANSFER SAVE is a good idea. Try to use as few new cells as possible.

If you just persist then you will find that you cannot do anything, such as BLANK or TRANSFER SAVE. You will just get an 'Insufficient Memory' message. But even then, there is one command you can still use, and very useful it is. That is DELETE. This can get you back to the previous stage when, although you were getting "0% Free", you could still use the commands. You can then TRANSFER SAVE again.

The purpose of TRANSFER SAVE is to break the work up into different worksheets, supporting and depending. You'll need to identify those parts of your old worksheet which belong naturally to the new dependent worksheet and which fall naturally into the new supporting worksheet. A major consideration will be the number of times you need to refer from one part to another.

NAMING

Introduction

In general naming is not concerned with making Multiplan *work*, only with making life easier if you're doing some complex things. You can skip it altogether and still produce exactly the same worksheet as though you had used naming. But you will often be more effective in your use of Multiplan if you employ this feature.

What it is

Naming is quite simply the ability to refer to a cell or group of cells by something, called a name, which remembers the Relative or Absolute Reference it had when you named it. This can contain Ranges, Intersections or Unions. It doesn't matter. It all gets remembered. If you look in the Full Reference Guide you will see many places where it says that you may enter a Relative or Absolute Reference or a Name.

Why use it?

There is not one single reason. If you use Naming you will do so for three possible reasons:

1. Your References will be easier to understand when you see statements like 'Pay+Bonus' instead of RC[−2]+RC[−1].

2. Having named a cell, you can GOTO it very quickly without having to look for it.

3. When you connect worksheets, using eXTERNAL COPY, naming is a convenient way of indicating which bit of the supporting worksheet you want copied into the depending one.

We'll now consider each one of these three reasons separately.

Readability

In a small worksheet the readability argument is often hard to justify. The advantage of using words that you are used to has to be weighed against the extra work of setting up the names. It's your decision. One argument you should not overlook: it all makes sense to you *now*. But when you come to use the worksheet in perhaps six months time and want to change part of it, will you be able to remember all that is in your mind now? If that thought worries you: you should be considering the use of names. We'll deal with how to do this soon.

A useful rule of thumb: if your worksheet extends over one screen, you'll probably need names. If it's less, you're better off without.

GOTO name

A common difficulty met by people new to Multiplan is that they spend a lot of time moving about the worksheet looking for the same place each time. This second use of naming is the answer to that problem. Just identify the place you're going to want to get to, name it, and GOTO name.

So if you have a table of results in Rows 38 to 49 and Columns 22 to 30, you can set up a name for the whole area. Then if you GOTO it you will find that the Cell Pointer immediately goes to R38C22. If you are going to print the whole table you can enter the same name when you supply the "area:" in the PRINT OPTIONS subcommand. Make sure you give a short and easy-to-remember name. That way you'll get the maximum benefit.

The same rule of thumb applies here: if your worksheet extends over one screen, you'll probably need names. If it's less, you're going to need it a lot less.

Connecting worksheets

The subject of connecting worksheets appears on page 45. The use of the NAME command in that connection is discussed here.

You do the linking of worksheets in the dependent worksheet. In that sheet you are prompted for the following information:

XTERNAL COPY from sheet: ▨▨▨   name: ▨▨▨   to: ▨▨▨
linked: Yes No

This means that you need to name the area in the supporting worksheet that is going to be copied into this dependent worksheet. So even if you have no other reason to name that area in the supporting worksheet, you now have one.

(Strictly speaking, you *don't* have to name it at all in order to connect worksheets! You could put an Absolute Reference in the place where you are prompted for a name. Clearly it can't be a Relative Reference, since the supporting worksheet has different References to where we are, in the dependent worksheet! However an Absolute Reference *may* be used. It still isn't a good idea though. The reason is that if you make a change in the supporting worksheet the Absolute Reference will be wrong, and the dependent worksheet will give no warning that it is wrong. If you use a name, all references will always be correct.)

Naming

When you enter the NAME command you will see the following message in the Command Line on your screen.

NAME   define name: ▨▨▨▨   to refer to: ▨▨▨▨

You're going to have complete flexibility over both the "define name:" field and the "to refer to:" field. We'll deal with each in turn.

Define your own names

The name that is going to be used has to be your own name: that way it will be meaningful to you. To define the name you may *either* key in the name you wish to give, *or* accept the name already in the field, *or* edit it.

How to enter names

If the Cell Pointer is over a cell with a text field in it, then you will be prompted with that field for "define name:". (By text we mean that it was entered with an ALPHA command.) This is a chance to make use of the most important feature of Multiplan: pointing. Note that you can use the contents of the text field to name not that cell but other cells nearby.

Permitted names

If you do enter the name you just key it in. There are a few simple rules:

* It *has* to begin with a letter.
* It *may not* include spaces.
* It may include *only*:

    letters;
    numbers, but they may not be the first character in the name;
    the . known as the period, but it may not come first;
    the _ known as the underscore, but it may not come first.

* It may *not* look like a reference to a row or column, like R3 or C49.
* It may not be more than 31 characters long, but you would be most unlikely to want to enter a name that long.

Although this looks like a long and worrying list it's usually pretty easy to keep within these rules without even being aware of them. If you break them you will be told of your mistake by seeing a #NAME message on the screen. You can then look at this list to find out why you got the message!

Upper case v. lower case

The way that Multiplan stores and compares these names ignores all consideration of upper and lower case. In fact you do not have to worry whether you are using upper or lower case.

'Capturing' a name

The reason why you are prompted with the contents of a cell if it contains text is so that you can 'capture' your own narrative and use it as a name. It must be text because, as we have just seen, you cannot use numbers as names. However, it is cells containing numbers that we really want to name so that we can use them in formulas. Multiplan has an answer to this.

Consider the following example:

	1	2	3	4	5	6	7
1		1980	1981	1982	1983	1984	
2	Costs						
3	Sales						
4		— — — — — — — — — — — — — — — — — — —					
5	Total						

If you place the Cell Pointer over R2C1 and enter 'Name', you will be prompted with the word 'Costs' in the "define name:" field. Consider the following steps:

1. You accept the word 'Costs' by 'tabbing' on to the next field.
2. In the next field which is "to refer to:" you will be prompted by the Cell Pointer's position, R2C1.
3. You *don't* accept it, but move the cell pointer to the right, to R2C2, under the year 1980.
4. You finish off by pressing the colon, :, and then pointing to R2C6 under the year 1984 and then pressing 'Return'.

Let's consider what we have just done. We have named the range R2C2:6 with the name 'Costs'. Notice that the narrative in the cell where the word 'Costs' appeared has been used again. This is important. You should realize that Multiplan is not unhappy about 'Costs' being the contents of one cell, and the name of another group of cells. That's no problem at all. But the important thing to remember is that you've used your own words and you'll have meaningful names when you use them in the future. And you did it, like you do all the best things in Multiplan, by pointing!

Vectors

If you now move the Cell Pointer to R3C1 and enter NAME the prompt will be something very smart. It will propose 'Sales' for the name and R3C2:6 for the reference. It remembers what you last did and applies it to the next Name you give. This will work for a line of cells along a row, or a whole row, or a line of cells down a column, or a whole column. These lines are called Vectors. You will certainly find this useful when you are using names in formulas while dealing with rows and columns of information.

Use of names

In the case of the example on the previous page what you can enter into R5C2 is 'Sales-Costs'. The *way* you do it is very helpful. Again, there is a choice of two methods. You can actually enter in the words. But this takes time and you might spell one of the words wrongly. The better way is by pointing. In this case you do it in the following way:

* Move the Cell Pointer to R5C2.
* Press '=' to show that you are going to enter a formula.
* Press the Function Key called 'reference'. (On the IBM PC it is F3.)
* Press the Right Arrow key: you will see one of the names that you have entered into this worksheet.
* Continue to press the arrow until you see the name you want: in this case it is 'Sales'.
* Now press the '−' sign.
* Now repeat the process for the second name, pressing 'Reference' and then the arrow until you see the name 'Costs'.
* Now press 'Return' and you have finished.

Having set up the formula which gives us a correct solution for 1980 we COPY RIGHT four cells from R5C2 which places the same formula in the total field for each year from 1980 onward. Note that all the formulas will look alike: 'Sales-Costs'. The correct answers will be produced for each year because Multiplan recognizes that Vectors with the same name need to be calculated again for each column (if the Vector is a row) or for each row (if the Vector is a column).

Referencing a single cell in a vector

You can even reference a single cell within a vector. Suppose that you need to use the Costs for 1984 in another formula. You may reference it in the following way:

'Costs C6'

Note that this is an **intersection** of the row containing the Vector 'Costs' with Column 6. The space between the word 'Costs' and the second reference, C6, is needed to show that this is not a single name 'CostsC6'. You may also refer to C6 relatively, that is as C[−1]. Note however that this has to be keyed in: you cannot use this feature with pointing.

Automatic editing of 'Captured' names

There may be some changes made to the names that you 'capture'. Because the rules for Names are much more strict than the rules for entering text, Multiplan will alter characters that it cannot accept as a name. Since only alphabetic, numeric, periods '.' and underscore '_' are permitted any non-permissible character is changed in the following way:

'.' period	comes through unchanged.
'_' underscore	comes through unchanged.
' ' space	comes through as underscore.
non-alphanumeric character	is dropped.
leading numeric character	is dropped.

A few examples should explain this process:

Text	Name
Year.1984	Year.1984
Year_1984	Year_1984
Year 1984	Year_1984
Year*1984	Year1984
=Year#1984	Year1984
1984Total	Total

You should beware of names such as 'Cost_of_Sales': they take some getting used to, but the benefit of having meaningful names outweighs this feeling of initial unfamiliarity.

Using names

Having set up our names let's consider the different ways in which they can be used. The following is a list of commands that use names:

BLANK	when you blank out a named area.
COPY	when you copy from or to a named area.
FORMAT	when you format a named area.
GOTO	when you GOTO a named area.
LOCK	when you lock or unlock a named area.
NAME	when you give a named area another name.
PRINT	when you print a named area.
VALUE	when you use names in formulas.
eXTERNAL	when you copy from a named area in the supporting worksheet.

PRINTING THE RESULTS

Introduction

Sooner or later we will want to print our worksheets. There's not much interest in just building a worksheet and seeing the results on the screen. Usually we want to print them out to show or to send to someone. It's not an easy subject to describe because we're not just talking about Multiplan but we're also talking about the sort of printer you use—and there are very many printers being used. But we're going to see how much help you can be given, although I don't know what kind of printer you have.

Concepts

Before we go into the way you use the PRINT command, we're going to look at the key concepts that we'll be using in explaining how to print. These concepts are:

* Margins.
* Printer setup.
* Printing formulas.
* Printing row-col numbers.

Margins

We're going to tell Multiplan how we want our information set out on the printed page. This will be the standard for every page in printing the active worksheet. Depending on the size of your worksheet you *could* be printing out several pages. A **page** in this context simply means what gets printed on one sheet, whether it has been split from a length of continuous stationery or was printed as a single sheet.

There are five different fields that you are going to have to specify:

*	Left	The margin on the left, meaning the spaces the printer places on the left of every line you are going to print.
*	Top	The margin at the top, meaning the blank lines the printer places on the top of every page you are going to print.
*	Print width	The number of printing positions across from the left margin.
*	Print length	The number of lines of print you want on each page starting at the top.
*	Page length	The number of printing lines there is space for on the printed page.

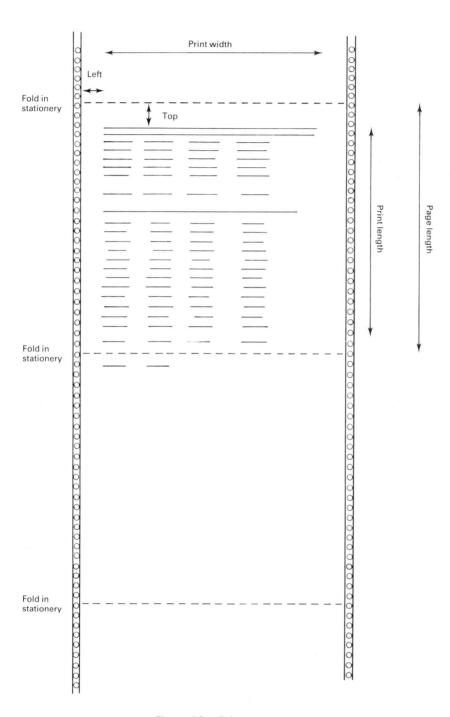

Figure 10   Print margins

Figure 10 shows how this appears on the stationery. Note that the first four are concerned with the **printing** of your document: the Page Length is only of interest to your printer so that it can know how far to 'throw' from one page to the next.

Printer Setup

Printers these days are very sophisticated. They can do so much . . . but they need to be told what to do. The Printer Setup is a way by which, through Multiplan, you can tell it to do a whole lot of things. Here are some examples:

* Print in condensed mode, meaning that you can print 132 characters on ordinary letter-width stationery.
* Print in double-strike mode, meaning that each character gets printed *twice*, for greater emphasis.
* Print in special character mode, such as in italics.

You will have to discover what codes are available and which of those you wish to use. This book cannot be more specific because the codes are different for different printers. But here are some examples for the Epson RX80 Printer. On this printer the examples mentioned above are generated by these sequences:

Condensed Mode	Alt 018	
Double-strike Mode	Alt 027	Alt 071
Select Special Characters	Alt 027	Alt 052

('Alt' means the 'Alternate' key.) To make use of these codes you will need to study the manual of the particular printer that you have.

Print formulas

Where there are formulas you normally see the **result** of the formula instead of the formula itself. That is usually what you want. Sometimes you would like to get a permanent copy of how you got those results, a copy which you can take away from the computer. You would be most likely to want to do this when you are developing your worksheet and are having problems with it. There is a 'Print Formulas' option which lets you see how the answers were got. It prints everything else normally but shows you the formulas, where there are any, as though you were looking at the Edit Line. In order to make room for the extra narrative all the columns are printed with twice the current column width.

Print row-col numbers

You can also specify that row and column numbers appear on your printout. This gives you a clear indication of the position of everything on the worksheet, and is the equivalent of what you see on the screen. You would also want to do this while developing your worksheet. Although the two can be used separately, people tend to require *either* formulas and row-col numbers *or* neither.

The PRINT command

The Print command has four fields:

PRINT: Printer File Margins Options

This command is used a little differently to the other commands. Here's how it works.

Print to File or Printer

The first decision that you make is whether to print to Printer or to File. Usually you'll be printing to the Printer. The Print to File option is placing an image of what you would have printed on to your diskette or hard disk. You'd do this so that it can be used later, for delayed printing or for use by a word-processing package. If you do print to file you'll be asked for a filename, so that the print image can later be identified by its name.

If you choose to print to the Printer, you'll need to consider the two other options first: PRINT MARGINS and PRINT OPTIONS. You enter those, and when you complete them you do *not* return to the main menu with the two command lines in the CONTROL AREA. You return to the Print Menu:

PRINT: Printer File Margins Options

This is because the PRINT sequence is not complete until you choose *either* File *or* Printer. You should enter both MARGINS and OPTIONS before printing unless you are certain that they are both correct.

Print Margins

The five fields are to be entered as follows:

PRINT MARGINS: left: ▒▒▒▒   top: ▒▒▒▒   print width: ▒▒▒▒
                    print length: ▒▒▒▒   page length: ▒▒▒▒

When you first enter PRINT MARGINS for a particular worksheet you are presented with the following defaults:

left: 5
top: 6
print width: 70
print length: 54
page length: 66

These defaults fit standard letter-sized stationery, but you have complete freedom to alter any or all of them. If you wish you may enter zero for both "left:" and "top:". All entries will be 'remembered' next time you print, provided that you SAVE the work-sheet after changing any parameters.

Print Options

The PRINT OPTIONS fields appear like this:

PRINT OPTIONS: area: ▓▓▓▓▓   setup: ▓▓▓▓▓
                        formulas: Yes No   row-col numbers: Yes No

There is no default for "setup", the defaults for "formulas:" and "row-col numbers:" are both 'No'. Be careful about the default for "area:". It seeks to anticipate what you want to print. Be sure to check it! It's not always correct.

The "area:" may be filled in by all these referencing choices: Relative and Absolute and Naming. You may use Intersections and Ranges, but not Unions. Pointing is recommended.

The characters that you put in "setup:" will look rather strange. Remember that they're not there for your benefit: they're talking to your printer in its own language.

These entries will be 'remembered' next time you print, provided that you SAVE the worksheet after changing them.

Printing areas larger than one page

In the PRINT command you will be specifying what you want to print. Often it will be an area that can fit onto one printed page. Sometimes you may have to arrange an area so that it can fit: often there are a few columns that can be reduced in width in order to fit everything in. But you need to understand what happens when you ask for an area larger than one page to be printed.

The 'page' we are discussing is the one that you specified with the PRINT MARGINS sub-command. What Multiplan does is to 'cut' your document up into units that can be printed, which you can then paste together into one large printed spreadsheet. It's useful to understand the sequence in which the 'cut' parts appear. Look at Figure 11. It shows that the pages work down the print area from top to bottom, and from left to right. Where there is only part of a page to print, a whole page is nevertheless printed. There is one exception to this: where one complete space for a page has *no* information in it, that page is not printed.

How Multiplan prints areas too large to be printed on one page

First page	Fifth page	Ninth page
Second page	Sixth page	Tenth page
Third page	Seventh page	Eleventh page
Fourth page	Eighth page	Twelfth page

Figure 11   Print sequence

PRINTING PROBLEMS

Non-adjacent areas

You may want to print alongside each other two areas that are not adjacent on the worksheet. The two areas may be placed next to each other on the screen by using WINDOW: you want to get them adjacent to each other on the printed page. Can Multiplan do this?

There is no automatic way of doing this: but it *can* be done. You cannot simply join the two areas in a Union by using a comma to link them together. By a series of COPYs and MOVEs you can put the two areas adjacent to each other and then specify the new total area in response to the "area:" field. Be careful to ensure that your formulas are still correct: you may have to edit some of them to correct them for their new positions.

Printing reports

We often use our Multiplan printouts either as reports or as parts of reports. It's a good idea to have properly lined-up reports with consecutive page numbers. One major advantage of Print to File is that a Word-processing Program can then do things like that for you. But you may not have access to a word-processing package.

If you do not use word processing you can take a few steps in Multiplan to make your results look more professional. You should organize your worksheet so that it will fit into the parameters that you specified with PRINT OPTIONS and PRINT MARGINS. Then you will not get odd pages with only a small amount of information on them. You can COPY the heading information to a new part of the worksheet, follow it by the information that didn't fit onto the first page and create your own page 2, with a new PRINT OPTIONS sub-command. It isn't difficult and the results will be a lot more impressive.

My printer doesn't work

If that is you problem you will have to go to the basics of your computer and your printer. Remember: it may have nothing to do with Multiplan. That isn't what this book is about. But here are a few questions to get you thinking:

* Is your printer switched on?

* Is your printer switched to manual control?

* Has your printer run out of paper?

* Is your printer connected to your computer?

* Is the "area:" in your PRINT OPTIONS sub-command referencing only empty cells?

SETTING UP A ROUTINE OPERATION

Introduction

If, when you have finished developing your worksheet, you wish to set it up so that someone else can enter the data as a routine operation then this section is intended to help you. You should aim to make this as easy as possible for someone who has no knowledge of your application.

You'll be making use of the following features:

LOCK CELLS
LOCK FORMULAS
The 'Next Unlocked Cell' Function Key

We'll look at each of these in turn and build up a routine operation. (These procedures are also relevant if you're going to enter your own data, but it's not going to be quite so important. You may well feel that you're going to spot any mistakes you make and therefore you won't need to take these measures. It's up to you.)

LOCK CELLS

Any cells that you do not want to be accidentally lost can be protected by the use of LOCK CELLS. Trying to change them causes a 'beep' and a 'Locked Cells may not be changed' message. You may use this in the case of some figures that you have entered. You know that they should not change or, if they do, you want to change them yourself. If you follow the procedure for LOCK CELLS, described in the Full Reference Guide, you will be able to protect them from your operator's accidental error. Make sure that the operator is not the kind of person who *wants* to unlock the cells! There is no way in Multiplan to stop that. Most operators I know wouldn't want to.

LOCK FORMULAS

Losing formulas is a serious business since they can be quite complex. The LOCK FORMULAS sub-command lets you protect all the formulas and all the text in a worksheet. Any attempt to alter them causes a 'beep' and a 'Locked Cells may not be changed' message. This way your operator can only change the cells that *you* want changed. So you make an area for entering the new sales information and the formulas produce the correct results. The narrative remains unchanged because LOCK FORMULAS applies to text as well as formulas. It is only numeric fields that you can change.

'Next Unlocked Cell' function key

A further aid in setting up your worksheet as a routine processing run is the 'Next Unlocked Cell' key. The idea is to set out the list of items on the worksheet in the same order as on the input document. That way your operator will enter an item, press 'Next Unlocked Cell', enter the next item and go through the document without having to line up the Cell Pointer at the correct position.

A worked example

We're going to consider a quite simple example which will illustrate the features described above. In this example we're going to assume that the operator's task is to enter information about a factory's attendance record:

	1	2	3	4	5	6	7
1		NORMAL	ACTUAL	VARIANCE			
2	DEPT	HOURS	HOURS	%			
3	– – – – – – – – – – – – – – –						
4	A	492	0	–100.00			
5	B	921	0	–100.00			
6	C	1062	0	–100.00			
7	D	503	0	–100.00			
8	– – – – – – – – – – – – – – –						
9	TOTALS	2978	0	–100.00			
10	– – – – – – – – – – – – – – –						

The formula in R4C4 is

(RC[–1]–RC[–2])/RC[–2]*100

This has been copied down to R5:7C4 and to R9C4. The formula in R9C2 is

SUM(R[–6]:R[–1]C)

This has been copied to R9C3. The –100.00 figures in Column 4 are because the current Actual Hours are all set at zero.

If you use LOCK FORMULAS then your operator cannot destroy R4:7C4 and R9C2:4, which contain formulas. You will also have protected all the narrative in Rows 1, 2, 3, 8, 9 and 10. And also the 'A', 'B', 'C' and 'D' in Column 1.

If you leave the Cell Pointer in R4C3 when the worksheet is SAVEd, then the operator will be prompted to start at the Actual Hours for Department A. If the 'Next Unlocked Cell' key is pressed after Actual Hours for Department A have been entered, then the Cell Pointer will immediately move down to R5C3.

Note that you must leave a zero in Row 4, 5, 6 and 7 of Column 4. Spaces will not do. If you don't do that the prompts will not reach those cells. It only works if cells have something in them, if only zero.

Locking some formulas

Sometimes you want to lock only some formulas, and not the others. Yet the LOCK FORMULAS sub-command only lets you lock all the formulas, not just some of them. There *is* an answer to this problem. The answer is:

Only enter the formulas you want to have locked.

Now LOCK FORMULAS.

Now enter more formulas: these, having been entered *after* the LOCK FORMULAS sub-command, will not be locked.

Written instructions

You should always give your operator written instructions on how to enter your data, and how to print out the results. A small example is given here showing an operator how to use the example we've just been looking at. The example is included so that you can develop your own version. It includes some ideas that it will pay you to think about. Remember, you cannot expect another person to have the same knowledge or interest that you have in your own worksheet.

SAMPLE GENERAL INSTRUCTIONS

1	NAME OF RUN	Monthly Attendance Analysis
2	worksheet NAME	Attend
3	DISK IDENTITY	MR96
4	FREQUENCY	Monthly
5	RUN DATE	Before the 7th of every month
6	SOURCE	Departmental form PN108
7	DISTRIBUTION	As on company list DST7
8	AUTHORITY	In case of difficulty consult R. Roper

SAMPLE OPERATIONAL STEPS

1   Load Multiplan Master Disk MP002.

2   Load Departmental Analysis Disk MR96.

3   Enter Multiplan by pressing MP80 from the main menu.

4   Load the worksheet by entering

      TRANSFER,

      LOAD,

      Right Arrow,

      point to the word ATTEND,

      press Return.

5   You are prompted to enter the Actual Hours for Department A. Enter it.

6   Press the "Next Unlocked Cells" Function Key.

7   Enter the return for Department B.
etc.

TEXT MANIPULATION

Multiplan has very good **text** capabilities. These are achieved by the use of the text functions and a relational operator, the & symbol.

What is text?

In Multiplan anything that has been entered with an ALPHA command is regarded as text. When you see it displayed in the Command Line you will see it enclosed by double quotes, ". These are used by Multiplan in order to recognize text fields. That is why you can never include double quotes within text fields.

It is important to realize that text and numbers behave in different ways: the rules governing each are different. For example: you can't do arithmetic on a text field, even if it contains a number that you entered using the ALPHA command.

In addition to being entered by the ALPHA command, text can be created by transforming numbers into text by using the text functions.

Text functions

We're going to consider the following functions, all of which deal with text.

FIXED
VALUE
DOLLAR
LEN
MID
REPT
&

FIXED

This function not only cuts down a value to the number of decimals that you specified but it also turns it into text. So if you have a number which is 957.724 and you enter a formula which is FIXED(Number,2) what you will get is "957.72" and you will not be able to do arithmetic with it. Unless the Alignment is 'Right' the amount will be left justified because it is text.

VALUE

The VALUE function has the opposite result to the FIXED function. If a text field is composed of digits that can produce a number (that is: numeric digits, a leading minus sign or $, or a number containing an E in scientific notation) then VALUE(X) will convert X into a numeric field on which you can do arithmetic.

LEN

The LEN function will tell you how many characters there are in a text field. So if R33C44 contains the word "Multiplan" the Function LEN(R33C44) will give the answer of 9.

MID

The MID function will extract a fixed portion of the text field. So in the previous example of the word "Multiplan" appearing in R33C44 we can enter the Function MID(R33C44,4,3). This will extract the three characters starting at the fourth: "tip".

REPT

The REPT function will generate a variable number of characters. There are two arguments. The first is the character that is to be repeated. The second is the number of times that it is to be repeated. REPT("*",10) will produce a set of 10 "*" characters. A more interesting use of this function is when we want to underline some text that appears in the row above. If we have the formula:

REPT("_",LEN(R[−1]C))

then we will be underlining the narrative above whatever length it is. Note that there are two left parentheses being balanced by two right parentheses.

&

We may also consider the use of the '&' symbol which acts as a concatenator on text fields. Suppose we wanted to place the word 'DOLLARS' *immediately* after a number, irrespective of its length.

Suppose the number to be in R14C39. The function could look like this:

FIXED(R14C39,2)&" DOLLARS"

Depending on the size of the numbers in R14C39 you could get these results:

390.00 DOLLARS
128946.98 DOLLARS
−3.91 DOLLARS
0.14 DOLLARS

These results are all left justified, which is the 'normal' Alignment for text. You can, however, change the alignment to right justification, in which case the result would be:

```
    390.00 DOLLARS
128946.98 DOLLARS
     -3.91 DOLLARS
      0.14 DOLLARS
```

USING WINDOWS

Introduction

Although you don't *have* to use windows, you'll find that large and complex work-sheets are a lot easier to manage if you use them. Properly used they can save you a lot of time.

What they are

With the use of windows you can split your screen into a number of different parts letting you look at different areas of your worksheet, these areas not usually being next to each other. For example, if you are altering assumptions, you'd like to see the total figure changing as you change the assumptions. That's fine if there is room on the screen for your assumptions and your total. If not, you'd need to keep moving down and back up again if you didn't have windows. With windows you can comfortably change things, play the 'what if' game, and see the results changing each time you alter one of the figures which go towards the total. Many people use it to keep an eye on the 'bottom line'. It does that very well.

Other new concepts

The following concepts all relate to windows:

* Windows.

* Titles.

* Scrolling.

* Linking.

* Borders.

* Window number.

* Window split.

Each are now described.

Windows

You *always* have at least one window. Whenever you start a new Multiplan session you will see the '#1' at the top left. That means 'Window number 1'. That's a good way of describing your screen, since it really is a window into your worksheet which may be a lot larger than can be fitted into one screen. The WINDOW commands are concerned with controlling the windows in your current worksheet.

Titles

A special form of window is called titles. This is where you want to see *both* the narrative at the top of a column *and* the narrative at the left of the row.

Scrolling

You can scroll whether you have windows or not. (Scrolling simply means causing your view of the worksheet to move in one of four directions—up, down, left or right.) The opportunities offered by scrolling become even more useful when you use windows. That's because you'll be able to arrange to scroll one set of information along with another.

Linking

When you scroll you may or may not want the window to scroll in harmony with some data outside the window. For example, your column headings go from 'January' to 'December' and there is not room for all of them across one screen. If you make the headings area a new window which is linked with the current window then you can scroll sideways—left and right—and always have the correct month appearing above the column even if you are more than a page down, in, say, Row 33.

Borders

A screen with windows in it can begin to look rather crowded. One way of distinguishing which is what is to get Multiplan draw a border round one or more of your windows. This will give your screen a very neat, clear appearance.

Remember, though, that the border takes up space on the worksheet. A horizontal border line occupies a row: meaning that you now can't have 20 rows on the screen, you're stuck with only 18, allowing for one line at the top and another at the bottom of your window. With vertical lines we lose, not a column, but one column-width position. It *can* mean that you have lost a whole column if the last one only just fitted in.

So, in deciding whether to have a border or not, you'll be weighing up the advantage of greater clarity against the disadvantage of less information on the screen. It's your decision.

Window number

Because we can have a maximum of eight different windows it is necessary to have some way of identifying which window we are referencing. For this purpose we have a window number which is displayed at the top left-hand corner with the '#1', '#2', etc. symbols.

THE FEATURES USED

The Multip an features we're now going to cover are:

WINDOW SPLIT HORIZONTAL
WINDOW SPLIT VERTICAL
WINDOW SPLIT TITLES
WINDOW BORDER
WINDOW CLOSE
'Next Window' Function Key
GOTO WINDOW

These are all explained individually below.

WINDOW SPLIT

The word 'split' is used because in order to create a new window, one of the old ones has to be split, remembering again that we always start with one window which is the whole worksheet. So we have to place the Cell Pointer in the position where we want the new window to appear. Then we must decide whether to split the window we're in (the active window) horizontally, vertically or both ways (titles).

The sequence of commands and sub-commands works like this:

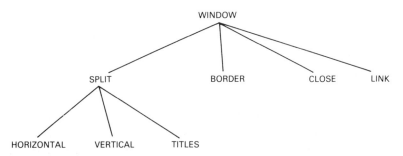

So, in order to split your windows, you must choose *two* sets of sub-commands. The sequence goes like this:

FIRST   Press 'W' for Window.

SECOND   Press 'S' for Split.

THIRD   Press 'V' for Vertical if you wish to create a vertical window. If you had wanted to split horizontally or titles then the third step would have been 'H' or 'T'.

The split

When you split a window a second area is created in which you can move about. Let's consider this example:

	1	2	3	4	5	6
1		January	February	March	April	May
2	— —					
3	Dept A					
4	Dept B					
5	Dept C					
6	Dept D					
7	Dept E					
	etc					
	etc					
	etc					
28	Dept Z					

You should understand that June will be in Column 7 and by the time we get to December we'll be looking at Column 13. There's not enough room for this table on one screen either horizontally or vertically. This is just what the WINDOW command is there to help with.

If you know you will need to scroll horizontally—across to the later part of the year—then it will be useful to SPLIT VERTICAL. Then you'll be able to see the 'Dept ' narrative all the way across to the right of the screen. If you know you will need to scroll vertically—down towards Dept Z—then it will be useful to SPLIT HORIZONTAL. Then you'll be able to see the 'Month' narrative all the way down the screen. If you want to do both, scroll right and left *and* up and down, then you can use the third option SPLIT TITLES. Using that, whichever way you scroll, you'll always be able to see which month and which Dept you're looking at.

When you have chosen whether you want to split vertically, horizontally or titles you'll be prompted by *two* questions:

where   The new window is to start:

        either row (if HORIZONTAL)
        or column (if VERTICAL)
        or row # and column # (if TITLES)

(Note the difference between row in HORIZONTAL and column in VERTICAL and row # and column # in TITLES. The first two are absolute row and column numbers. The last two, signified with a #, are relative to the top left of the active window.)

linked   Meaning whether the new window is to be linked with the old one.

We'll now consider each of these questions:

Where

When you indicate where you want the split to take place, you'll be prompted by the **active** row or column number. That means you'll be able to accept this proposed response if you've remembered to position your Cell Pointer before you entered 'W' for Window. Of course, you can always change the number by not accepting the proposed response and entering a different one of your own.

The new window will start *on* the chosen row or column number. For example, if you decide to SPLIT HORIZONTAL the chosen row will be the *first* row in the new window. You'll see an 'Illegal Parameter' Error Message if you try to make an impossible split, like having the Cell Pointer in R1C1: if this happens there's nothing to split.

If the window being split has a border then both of the new windows will have borders.

Linked

Linking is the ability to get the two windows (the old and the new) to scroll in harmony with each other. If you specify linking for a HORIZONTAL SPLIT then, in the example we looked at, if you scroll to the right then months will move along in line with the data for those months.

You'll generally specify 'Yes' for linking whenever you have descriptions either as headings or narrative on the left. You'll specify 'No' when you have just an independent part of the worksheet, for example, the bottom line.

When you link windows the new window will not have its own column or row descriptions. This is to avoid wasting space on the screen. With unlinked windows the new window requires this information, but with linked windows it's not needed.

When you SPLIT TITLES you are *not* prompted with the 'linked' question because TITLES are *always* linked.

Window numbers

Your window numbers will be assigned automatically by Multiplan: there's no need to do anything about them. This explanation is included just so that you will know what is happening and why.

Every time you split a window a new window is created, the window number being one greater than the previous one. When you create your first window, you'll be in Window #1. The new one will be Window #2. You're always creating a new window by splitting an old one. So if there are already four windows and you split Window #2, then the new window must be Window #5. The window number will appear at the top left of each window. In the active window the window marker is highlighted.

BORDER

The message on your screen appears:

WINDOW change border in window number: ▓▓▓▓

You are prompted with the active window number. It pays to position the Cell Pointer in the window where you want to change the border. You may also change the window number in the prompt.

The message says "change border in window number:". This is because you do not have one sub-command for putting a border *on* and another for taking it *off*. The status changes every time you issue a sub-command which is opposite to the present one. If you have a border and want to lose it, use WINDOW BORDER. If you don't have a border and want to get one, also use WINDOW BORDER.

CLOSE

WINDOW CLOSE is the opposite of WINDOW SPLIT. You are asked to supply the window number of the window that needs to be closed. The active window number is proposed. It pays to move the Cell Pointer to the window you want to close before entering WINDOW CLOSE. But you may alter the window number in the proposed response.

When windows are closed the area becomes part of the windows from which they were originally split. All the splits are remembered by Multiplan. So if you are closing Window #4 it will be absorbed into the window from which Window #4 was split. All the window numbers which are greater than the one that you have removed will now be renumbered as one less. You cannot close Window #1, because there must always be one window.

LINK

WINDOW LINK lets you set up or remove links between a pair of windows. You may not need this feature, since you'll usually be completing the "link:" field in WINDOW SPLIT. But Multiplan lets you change your mind. That's where WINDOW LINK comes in.

The message on your screen appears:

WINDOW LINK   window number: ▓▓▓▓   with window number: ▓▓▓▓
                       linked: Yes No

You are now able to set up *or* remove a link between two windows. The same sub-command is used for both actions.

The proposed response for the first window number will be the active window number. It pays to position the Cell Pointer correctly before issuing the sub-command. You can also change the proposed window number. The second window stated will be the *most likely* window number. Look carefully: it might not be correct. The rules for deciding which second window will be proposed depends on what splits have taken place. If you enter a second window which cannot be linked with the first (if they are not adjacent) then you will receive a 'Cannot link those windows' message.

You use this sub-command to make a link and also to undo it. You simply change the "Yes No" entry in the third field. But you can only undo a link made with the WINDOW LINK sub-command. If it was made by the WINDOW SPLIT sub-command then you will have to CLOSE the window and then SPLIT it again, this time choosing the 'unlinked' option.

Next Window key

You also need to be able to move the Call Pointer from one window to another: to change the active window. You have a 'Next Window' key for this purpose. On the IBM PC this is F1. It moves you from the active window number to the next numerically greater number. So, if the active window number is #3 then pressing this key once will get you to Window #4. When you have reached the highest window number that has been opened you can go on to Window #1 by pressing the 'Next Window' key once more.

GOTO WINDOW

You'll usually prefer to use the 'Next Window' key rather than the GOTO WINDOW sub-command. In GOTO WINDOW the message on your screen will be:

GOTO WINDOW   window number: row: column:

If you do use GOTO WINDOW you'll find that the proposed response will move the active cell to the upper left of the window (and of the screen if the active window is #1). This is fine if you want to reorganize your screen that way. But it won't get you to another window. If you alter the proposed window to the one you want you still have to think about correcting the responses to the "row:" and "column:" fields. The proposed responses give the position of the active cell in the active window but it's not very likely that this row:column combination in the target window will be where you want to go. Often it won't be what you want, and if you go there you'll notice all the useful information disappearing from the target window. That won't happen if you use the 'Next Window' key.

PART 3
FULL REFERENCE GUIDE

Introduction

In this part you will find easily located data about each of the commands and sub-commands. Because the pages have a uniform structure you know just where to find the information you need. The filing sequence is commands in alphabetic order and the sub-commands in alphabetic order within their commands.

This sequence is illustrated here:

The sub-commands are entered by first entering the commands. Where it is needed a new menu appears showing you which sub-commands you may enter for that command.

Note that in the case of the FORMAT DEFAULT and WINDOW SPLIT there is a second level of sub-command to enter before you may enter the information required in the fields. Multiplan does not recognize 'sub-sub-commands'—what is not a command is a sub-command.

The Full Reference Guide seeks to assist you in your use of these commands and sub-commands. In many cases you will find enough information here without needing to look elsewhere. Where it is relevant the pages of information will, against the REFERENCE narrative, suggest where else you may look in this book.

You will soon become accustomed to the uniform structure of the pages in this Guide: this will make it easier for you to find what you are looking for. You will be told the precise effect of each command, what its likely uses are and any warning and advice that is relevant. There is generally a proposed response in Multiplan, and this Guide will advise you about the occasions when you can use it, thus saving you time.

In addition to the other references you may also use the Quick Reference Guide to assist you if you are unsure about the meaning of any particular word.

FULL REFERENCE GUIDE

WHAT IT DOES	**Command**	**ALPHA**

PURPOSE

To enter text into the worksheet.

RESULTS

CONTENTS	Previous contents replaced by new alpha text.
FORMAT	No change to existing format but text will conform to alignment and format code.
FORMULA	Any formula in the cell is lost.
LOCKING	You cannot enter text into cells that are locked.
NAME	Entering text causes no change to the name.

LIKELY USES

To identify the information you have on your worksheet, as in the case of a label at the top of a column.

REFERENCES

Data Representation, page 43.
Text Functions, page 103.
Extended Entry, page 136.

WARNINGS

Make sure you select the ALPHA command first. The most common mistake in Multiplan is to forget to do this. Then if your text begins with the letter 'O' Multiplan will immediately put you into the OPTIONS command!

Sometimes numbers have to be entered as text (for example, dates). These have to be entered with the ALPHA command. If you try to use these in formulas you will not be able to do so. You can usually convert them to numeric format using the VALUE function.

HOW TO USE IT	Command	ALPHA

TO SELECT THIS COMMAND:

either   Press A or A.

or   Because the Command Cursor is always pointing to 'A' at the beginning of a Command, you may just press 'Return'.

or   Press space bar (and backspace) until the Command Cursor is over the word 'Alpha' and then press 'Return'.

THE COMMAND MENU:

COMMAND LINE   ALPHA:

MESSAGE LINE   Enter text (no double quotes).

This means: You may enter text into the active cell or edit the text that is already there. Your text may not include double quotes, '', because that is used by Multiplan to identify text.

PROPOSED RESPONSE   The current contents of the active cell are shown in the Command Line. If you want to enter text this is no use to you, but if you want to edit it you can now go ahead.

OTHER RESPONSES   You will be *either* entering text *or* editing the text that is already there.

ENTERING TEXT   You may now use any key to insert text, *except* the '' (double quote) key. This you will have to do without.

EDITING TEXT   To edit the text that is already in the Command Line you will use the same keys in the same way as when using the EDIT command. You may also edit the text that you are now entering in the same way.

COMPLETION   When you have finished entering or editing the text in the Command Line you accept it by pressing 'Return'.

EXTENDED ENTRY   When you are entering information into a series of cells, whether text or numeric, you may speed up the task by going into Extended Entry mode which is explained on page 136.

WHAT IT DOES	Command	BLANK

PURPOSE

To empty out the contents of a cell or a group of cells.

RESULTS

CONTENTS	Cells will now contain spaces.
FORMAT	No change.
FORMULA	Any formula in the cell or cells is lost.
LOCKING	You cannot BLANK cells that are locked.
NAME	No change.

LIKELY USES

To correct mistakes or to set cells back to a starting position, for instance at the start of a new accounting period.

WARNINGS

Avoid confusion between BLANK and DELETE and TRANSFER CLEAR.

DELETE will completely remove the specified cells (including their formats) from the worksheet.

TRANSFER CLEAR will remove the whole worksheet.

BLANK will simply set the specified cells back to nothing but leave the rest of the worksheet unchanged.

HOW TO USE IT	**Command**	**BLANK**

TO SELECT THIS COMMAND: either Press B or b.

or Press space bar (and backspace) until the Command Cursor is over the word 'Blank' and then press 'Return'.

THE COMMAND MENU:

   COMMAND LINE   BLANK cells:

   MESSAGE LINE   Enter reference to cell or group of cells.

   This means: You can choose what area of cells to blank out.

PROPOSED RESPONSE   The Command Cursor is pointing at the active cell. Press 'Return' to blank it out.

OTHER RESPONSE   You may insert your own reference and also edit the proposed response. The response may be an Absolute Reference or a Name. Press 'Return' to accept the response.

COMPLETION   When you have pressed 'Return' the command is complete.

WHAT IT DOES	**Command**	**COPY**

PURPOSE

To copy values, text or formulas from certain cells to other cells.

RESULTS

The receiving cells will obtain their information from the sending cells. The following comments relate to what will happen in the receiving cells.

CONTENTS	The receiving cell will take the text or value from the sending cell but not if the sending cell has a formula.
FORMAT	The receiving cell will now have the Alignment and Format Code of the sending cell. But the column width does not change.
FORMULA	The receiving cell will take its formula from the sending cell.
LOCKING	You cannot COPY into a locked cell. You may copy *from* a locked cell.
NAME	NAMEd cells may be copied, but the receiving area does not take the name of the sending area.

LIKELY USES

This is the key command in building up a worksheet because it copies formulas while ensuring that the new formulas are relatively correct in their new positions.

REFERENCES

Reasons for Relative Referencing, page 13.

WARNING

Make sure that the receiving cells do not contain information that you need to keep.

ADVICE

Look for opportunities to use COPY: it will certainly save you time in building your worksheet.

HOW TO USE IT	**Command**	**COPY**

TO SELECT THIS COMMAND:

either	Press C or c.
or	Press space bar (and backspace) until the Command Cursor is over the word 'Copy' and then press 'Return'.

THE COMMAND MENU:

COMMAND LINE   COPY: Right Down From

MESSAGE LINE   Select Option or type command letter.

This means: You can choose from the three sub-commands the exact method you wish to use for copying.

METHODS OF COPYING

The difference between the three methods of copying is as follows:

COPY RIGHT means copying from a cell (or adjacent cells along a column, or a whole column) to a cell or cells immediately to the right.

COPY DOWN means copying from a cell (or adjacent cells along a row, or a whole row) to a cell or cells immediately underneath.

COPY FROM is used for any other sort of copying.

PROPOSED RESPONSE

The Command Cursor is pointing at 'Right'. Press 'Return' to 'Copy Right'.

OTHER RESPONSES

You may select the correct sub-command by ONE of the following methods:

either	Press R (or r) or D (or d) or F (or f).
or	Press space bar (and backspace) until the Command Cursor is over the required word, 'Right' or 'Down' or 'From'. Then press 'Return'.

THE NEXT STEP

You are now presented with the sub-menu which relates to the sub-command which you have chosen. Each is explained in the following pages.

ILLUSTRATED EXAMPLES   Sub-command   COPY DOWN

FOUR TYPES OF RESPONSE

COPY DOWN 1 POSITION FROM 1 CELL

Copies down from the sending
cell to the receiving cell.

Example: COPY DOWN number of cells: 1 starting at: R15C30

COPY DOWN MORE THAN 1 POSITION FROM 1 CELL

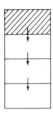

Copies down the same information from the one cell
into *each* of the receiving cells.

Example: COPY DOWN number of cells: 3 starting at: R15C30

COPY DOWN 1 POSITION FROM A GROUP OF CELLS

Copies from each cell in the sending
row to the cell with the corresponding
position in the receiving row.

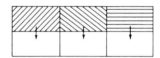

Example: COPY DOWN number of cells: 1 starting at: R15C30:32

COPY DOWN MORE THAN 1 POSITION FROM A GROUP OF CELLS

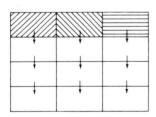

Copies from each cell in the sending row to the cell
with a corresponding position in the receiving rows.

Example: COPY DOWN number of cells: 3 starting at: R15C30:32

HOW TO USE IT	Sub-command	COPY DOWN

THE SUB-MENU:

COMMAND LINE

COPY DOWN number of cells: ▓▓▓▓
starting at: ▓▓▓

MESSAGE LINE

Enter a number.

This means:

You may choose how many cells you will copy down and from where you will start.

PROPOSED RESPONSE

If you have already used COPY DOWN or COPY RIGHT in this session on this worksheet the "number of cells:" will show the number of cells copied last time. Otherwise it will be blank. The "starting at:" field will give the reference of the active cell.

To COPY DOWN from the Active Cell the number of cells stated in the Command Line, just press 'Return'.

OTHER RESPONSES

You may use the entries in the two fields in this sub-menu to COPY DOWN by entering the information as stated below.

See the illustration on the page opposite.

THE TWO FIELDS

In each of these two fields you will be *either* accepting the entry already there by 'tabbing' on to the next field, *or* making an entry of your own, *or* editing the entry that is already in the field. As soon as you see a set of two correct responses you can leave the command by pressing the 'Return' key.

FIRST FIELD

number of cells: The number required is the number of positions that you want the starting point copied down.

SECOND FIELD

starting at: Enter the reference to the cell or cells that are the starting point of the COPY DOWN sub-command. This may be a Relative or Absolute Reference or a Name. The starting point must be either a single cell, or a group of adjacent cells along a row, or a whole row.

COMPLETION

When both fields are correct you accept them by pressing 'Return'.

ILLUSTRATED EXAMPLES   Sub-command   COPY FROM

FOUR TYPES OF RESPONSE

COPY FROM A CELL TO A CELL

Copies from the sending cell to
the receiving cell.

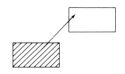

COPY FROM A CELL TO A GROUP OF CELLS

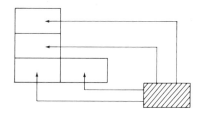

Copies the same information from the
one cell into *each* of the receiving cells.

COPY FROM A GROUP OF CELLS TO A CELL

The 'shape' of the sending
group is copied over to the
receiving area. The referenced
single cell fixes the top left
corner of the receiving area. Copies
from each cell in the sending area
to the cell with the corresponding
position in the receiving area.

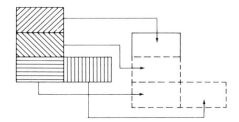

COPY FROM A GROUP OF CELLS TO A GROUP OF CELLS

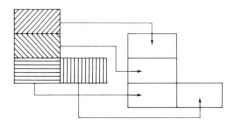

Copies from each cell in the sending
area to the cell with a corresponding
position in the receiving area. Multiplan
checks that the two 'shapes' are
identical. If they are not you will get an
'Illegal Parameter' message.

The group of cells may be an Absolute or Relative Reference or a Name. Its shape may be any
sort of shape, including a column or a row.

HOW TO USE IT	Sub-command	COPY FROM

THE SUB-MENU:

COMMAND LINE — COPY FROM cells: ░░░░ to cells: ░░░░

MESSAGE LINE — Enter reference to cell or group of cells.

This means: — You may copy from any area of the worksheet to any other area.

If the sending area is one cell its contents will be copied to all the cells in the receiving area.

If the sending area is greater than one cell, each cell in the sending area is copied to a corresponding cell in the receiving area. If only one cell is referenced for the receiving area it will take its shape from the sending area and its position from the reference, giving it its top left corner.

PROPOSED RESPONSE — The "cells:" and "to cells:" fields on the screen will both give the reference of the active cell.

You would not accept the proposed response without modification since it would simply copy the active cell to itself.

OTHER RESPONSES — You may use the entries in the two fields in this sub-menu to COPY FROM by entering the information as stated below.

See the illustration on the page opposite.

THE TWO FIELDS — In each of these two fields you will be *either* accepting the entry already there by 'tabbing' on to the next field, *or* making an entry of your own, *or* editing the entry that is already in the field. As soon as you see a set of two correct responses you can leave the command by pressing the 'Return' key.

FIRST FIELD — cells: Enter here a reference that correctly describes the sending area. You may use a Relative or Absolute Reference, or a Name.

SECOND FIELD — to cells: Enter the reference that correctly describes the receiving area. You are advised to use the method of referencing the top left corner of the receiving area: the third example on the opposite page.

COMPLETION — When both fields are correct you accept them by pressing 'Return'.

ILLUSTRATED EXAMPLES   Sub-command   COPY RIGHT

FOUR TYPES OF RESPONSE

COPY RIGHT 1 POSITION FROM 1 CELL

Copies right from the sending
cell to the receiving cell.

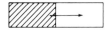

Example: COPY RIGHT number of cells: 1 starting at: R15C30

COPY RIGHT MORE THAN 1 POSITION FROM 1 CELL

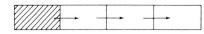

Copies right the same information from
the one cell into *each* of the receiving
cells.

Example: COPY RIGHT number of cells: 3 starting at: R15C30

COPY RIGHT 1 POSITION FROM A GROUP OF CELLS

Copies from each cell in the
sending column to the cell with
the corresponding position
in the receiving column.

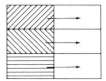

Example: COPY RIGHT number of cells: 1 starting at: R15:17C30

COPY RIGHT MORE THAN 1 POSITION FROM A GROUP OF CELLS

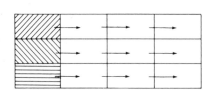

Copies from each cell in the sending
column to the cell with a corresponding
position in the receiving column.

Example: COPY RIGHT number of cells: 3 starting at: R15:17C30

HOW TO USE IT	**Sub-command**	**COPY RIGHT**

THE SUB-MENU:

COMMAND LINE | COPY RIGHT number of cells: starting at:

MESSAGE LINE | Enter a number.

This means: | You may choose how many cells you will copy right and from where you will start.

PROPOSED RESPONSE | If you have already used COPY RIGHT or COPY DOWN in this session on this worksheet the "number of cells:" will show the number of cells copied last time. Otherwise it will be blank. The "starting at:" field will give the reference of the active cell.

To COPY RIGHT from the Active Cell the number of cells stated in the Command Line, just press 'Return'.

OTHER RESPONSES | You may use the entries in the two fields in this sub-menu to COPY RIGHT by entering the information as stated below.

See the illustration on the page opposite.

THE TWO FIELDS | In each of these two fields you will be *either* accepting the entry already there by 'tabbing' on to the next field, *or* making an entry of your own, *or* editing the entry that is already in the field. As soon as you see a set of two correct responses you can leave the command by pressing the 'Return' key.

FIRST FIELD | number of cells: | The number required is the number of positions that you want the starting point copied to the right.

SECOND FIELD | starting at: | Enter the reference to the cell or cells that are the starting point of the COPY RIGHT sub-command. This may be a Relative or Absolute Reference or a Name. The starting point must be either a single cell, or a group of adjacent cells along a column, or a whole column.

COMPLETION | When both fields are correct you accept them by pressing 'Return'.

WHAT IT DOES	**Command**	**DELETE**

PURPOSE To remove certain cells from the worksheet.

RESULTS The specified cells will disappear from the worksheet. New cells will move in to replace the deleted ones, from right to left if you are deleting columns and from bottom to top if you are deleting rows. All references are recalculated.

CONTENTS	All the contents of the selected cells are lost.
FORMAT	All the formats of the selected cells are lost.
FORMULA	All the formulas of the selected cells are lost.
LOCKING	Locked cells may be DELETEd.
NAME	NAMEd cells may be DELETEd. Any references to names which reference areas completely DELETEd cause a #NAME error message.

LIKELY USES You would use it, for example, if you wish to remove all mention of a product that is no longer supplied.

WARNINGS If you DELETE a row or column that contains the end of a range you will get a #REF message. See 'Breaking the Range', page 28 on how to prevent this.

Remember that other cells will move into the positions previously occupied by the DELETEd cells. These new cells could have formats, values and formulas that you did not expect.

Any cells brought in off the end of the worksheet to fill the space made available will have default formats.

ADVICE Consider carefully whether you really want to use BLANK rather than DELETE.

DELETE will completely remove the specified cells (including their formats) from the worksheet.

TRANSFER CLEAR will remove the whole worksheet. BLANK will simply set the specified cells back to nothing but leave the rest of the worksheet unchanged.

Remember that you do not have to delete whole rows or columns.

HOW TO USE IT	**Command**	**DELETE**

TO SELECT THIS COMMAND: either Press D or d.

or Press space bar (and backspace) until the Command Cursor is over the word 'Delete' and then press 'Return'.

THE COMMAND MENU:

COMMAND LINE DELETE: Row Column

MESSAGE LINE Select Option or type command letter.

This means: You can choose from the two sub-commands whether to delete row or columns.

PROPOSED RESPONSE The Command Cursor is pointing at 'Row'. Press 'Return' to delete rows.

OTHER RESPONSES You may select the correct sub-command by ONE of the following methods:

either Press R (or r) or C (or c).

or Press space bar (and backspace) until the Command Cursor is over the required word, 'Row' or 'Column'. Then press 'Return'.

THE NEXT STEP You are now presented with the sub-menu which relates to the sub-command which you have chosen. Each is explained in the following pages.

ILLUSTRATED EXAMPLE   **Sub-command**   **DELETE COLUMN**

An example of the way that the DELETE COLUMN sub-command works is illustrated on this page.

```
     31      32      33      34      35      36      37      38      39      40
61   \\\\\\\\\\\\\\\\]]]]]]]]]]]]]]]]]]]//////////////////
62   \\\\\\\\\\\\\\\\]]]]]]]]]]]]]]]]]]]//////////////////
63   \\\\\\\\\\\\\\\\]]]]]]]]]]]]]]]]]]]//////////////////
64   \\\\\\\\\\\\\\\\]]]]]]]]]]]]]]]]]]]//////////////////
65   \\\\\\\\\\\\\\\\]]]]]]]]]]]]]]]]]]]//////////////////
66   \\\\\\\\\\\\\\\\]]]]]]]]]]]]]]]]]]]//////////////////
67   \\\\\\\\\\\\\\\\]]]]]]]]]]]]]]]]]]]//////////////////
68   \\\\\\\\\\\\\\\\]]]]]]]]]]]]]]]]]]]//////////////////
69   \\\\\\\\\\\\\\\\]]]]]]]]]]]]]]]]]]]//////////////////
70
71                      ILLUSTRATION BEFORE DELETION
```

Suppose that we now select DELETE COLUMN and that the sub-menu fields are entered as follows. The result is shown immediately below.

DELETE COLUMN   # no of columns: 3   starting at: 34
                  between rows: 1 and : 255

```
     31      32      33      34      35      36      37      38      39      40
61   \\\\\\\\\\\\\\\\\///////////////////
62   \\\\\\\\\\\\\\\\\///////////////////
63   \\\\\\\\\\\\\\\\\///////////////////
64   \\\\\\\\\\\\\\\\\///////////////////
65   \\\\\\\\\\\\\\\\\///////////////////
66   \\\\\\\\\\\\\\\\\///////////////////
67   \\\\\\\\\\\\\\\\\///////////////////
68   \\\\\\\\\\\\\\\\\///////////////////
69   \\\\\\\\\\\\\\\\\///////////////////
70
71              ILLUSTRATION AFTER DELETING WHOLE COLUMNS
```

But, if the DELETE COLUMN sub-menu selections on the original worksheet had been as follows, then the result would have been:

DELETE COLUMN   # no of columns: 3   starting at: 34
                  between rows: 64 and : 66

```
     31      32      33      34      35      36      37      38      39      40
61   \\\\\\\\\\\\\\\\]]]]]]]]]]]]]]]]]]]//////////////////
62   \\\\\\\\\\\\\\\\]]]]]]]]]]]]]]]]]]]//////////////////
63   \\\\\\\\\\\\\\\\]]]]]]]]]]]]]]]]]]]//////////////////
64   \\\\\\\\\\\\\\\\\///////////////////
65   \\\\\\\\\\\\\\\\\///////////////////.
66   \\\\\\\\\\\\\\\\\///////////////////
67   \\\\\\\\\\\\\\\\]]]]]]]]]]]]]]]]]]]//////////////////
68   \\\\\\\\\\\\\\\\]]]]]]]]]]]]]]]]]]]//////////////////
69   \\\\\\\\\\\\\\\\]]]]]]]]]]]]]]]]]]]//////////////////
70
71              ILLUSTRATION AFTER DELETING PART OF COLUMNS
```

HOW TO USE IT   Sub-Command   DELETE COLUMN

THE SUB-MENU:

COMMAND LINE	DELETE COLUMN # of columns: 1 starting at: ▦ between rows: 1 and : 255
MESSAGE LINE	Enter a number.
This means:	You may choose which columns to delete, and whether to include whole or partial columns.

PROPOSED RESPONSE

The "starting at:" field on your screen will state the column number where your Cell Pointer is placed at the moment. The "# of columns:", "between rows:" and "and:" are all as shown above.

To DELETE the Column on which the Cell Pointer is placed, just press 'Return'. This will often be what you want to do.

OTHER RESPONSES

You may use the entries in the four fields in this sub-menu to DELETE:

either   One or more than one column.

or   Part of a column or more than one column.

See the illustration on the page opposite.

THE FOUR FIELDS	In each of these four fields you will be *either* accepting the number already there by 'tabbing' on to the next field, *or* entering a number of your own. As soon as you see a set of four correct responses you can leave the command by pressing the 'Return' key.
FIRST FIELD	# of columns: Enter the number of columns you wish to delete unless 1 is correct.
SECOND FIELD	Starting at: Enter the number of the first column you wish to DELETE unless the correct column number is present.
THIRD FIELD	between rows: Enter the first row number of the columns you wish to delete unless 1 is correct.
FOURTH FIELD	and: Enter the last row number of the columns you wish to delete unless 255 is correct.
COMPLETION	When all four fields are correct you accept them by pressing 'Return'.

ILLUSTRATED EXAMPLE   Sub-command   DELETE ROW

An example of the way that the DELETE ROW sub-command works is illustrated on this page.

```
     1     2     3     4     5     6     7     8     9    10
 1   \\\\\\\\\\\\\\\\\\\\\\\\\\\\\\\\\\\\\\\\\\\\\\\\\\\\\\\\\\\\
 2   \\\\\\\\\\\\\\\\\\\\\\\\\\\\\\\\\\\\\\\\\\\\\\\\\\\\\\\\
 3   \\\\\\\\\\\\\\\\\\\\\\\\\\\\\\\\\\\\\\\\\\\\\\\\\\\\\\\\\\
 4   ]]]]]]]]]]]]]]]]]]]]]]]]]]]]]]]]]]]]]]]]]]]]]]]]]]]]]]
 5   ]]]]]]]]]]]]]]]]]]]]]]]]]]]]]]]]]]]]]]]]]]]]]]]]]]]]
 6   ]]]]]]]]]]]]]]]]]]]]]]]]]]]]]]]]]]]]]]]]]]]]]]]]]]]]]]
 7   ///////////////////////////////////////////////////////
 8   ///////////////////////////////////////////////////////
 9   ///////////////////////////////////////////////////////
10
11              ILLUSTRATION BEFORE DELETION
```

Suppose that we now select DELETE ROW and that the sub-menu fields are entered as follows. The result is shown immediately below.

DELETE ROW   # no of rows: 3   starting at: 4
              between columns: 1 and : 63

```
     1     2     3     4     5     6     7     8     9    10
 1   \\\\\\\\\\\\\\\\\\\\\\\\\\\\\\\\\\\\\\\\\\\\\\\\\\\\\\\\\\\\
 2   \\\\\\\\\\\\\\\\\\\\\\\\\\\\\\\\\\\\\\\\\\\\\\\\\\\\\\\\
 3   \\\\\\\\\\\\\\\\\\\\\\\\\\\\\\\\\\\\\\\\\\\\\\\\\\\\\\\\\\
 4   ///////////////////////////////////////////////////////
 5   ///////////////////////////////////////////////////////
 6   ///////////////////////////////////////////////////////
 7
 8
 9
10
11          ILLUSTRATION AFTER DELETING WHOLE ROWS
```

But, if the DELETE ROW sub-menu selections on the original worksheet had been as follows, then the result would have been:

DELETE ROW   # no of rows: 3   starting at: 4
              between columns: 3 and :7

```
     1     2     3     4     5     6     7     8     9    10
 1   \\\\\\\\\\\\\\\\\\\\\\\\\\\\\\\\\\\\\\\\\\\\\\\\\\\\\\\\\\\\
 2   \\\\\\\\\\\\\\\\\\\\\\\\\\\\\\\\\\\\\\\\\\\\\\\\\\\\\\\\
 3   \\\\\\\\\\\\\\\\\\\\\\\\\\\\\\\\\\\\\\\\\\\\\\\\\\\\\\\\\\
 4   ]]]]]]]]]]]////////////////////////////////]]]]]]]]]]
 5   ]]]]]]]]]]]////////////////////////////////]]]]]]]]]]
 6   ]]]]]]]]]]]////////////////////////////////]]]]]]]]]]
 7   //////////                              //////////
 8   //////////                              //////////
 9   //////////                              //////////
10
11          ILLUSTRATION AFTER DELETING PART OF ROWS
```

HOW TO USE IT   Sub-command   DELETE ROW

THE SUB-MENU:

COMMAND LINE

DELETE ROW # of rows: 1 starting at:
                        between columns: 1 and : 63

MESSAGE LINE

Enter a number.

This means:

You may choose which rows to delete and whether to include whole or partial rows.

PROPOSED RESPONSE

The "starting at:" field on your screen will state the row number where your cell pointer is placed at the moment. The "# of rows:", "between columns:" and "and:" are all as shown above.

To DELETE the Row on which the Cell Pointer is placed, just press 'Return;. This will often be what you want to do.

OTHER RESPONSES

You may use the entries in the four fields in this sub-menu to DELETE:

either   One or more than one row.

or   Part of a row or more than one row.

See the illustration on the page opposite.

THE FOUR FIELDS

In each of these four fields you will be *either* accepting the number already there by 'tabbing' on to the next field, *or* entering a number of your own. As soon as you see a set of four correct responses you can leave the command by pressing the 'Return' key.

FIRST FIELD

# of rows: Enter the number of rows you wish to delete unless 1 is correct.

SECOND FIELD

starting at: Enter the number of the first row you wish to DELETE unless the correct row number is present.

THIRD FIELD

between columns: Enter the first column of the rows you wish to delete unless 1 is correct.

FOURTH FIELD

and: Enter the last column number of the rows you wish to delete unless 63 is correct.

COMPLETION

When all four fields are correct you accept them by pressing 'Return'.

WHAT IT DOES	**Command**	**EDIT**

PURPOSE	To alter the contents of the active cell without having to enter all of it again.	
RESULTS	CONTENTS	You use EDIT to alter the contents.
	FORMAT	No change.
	FORMULA	You use EDIT to alter a formula.
	LOCKING	You cannot edit a locked cell.
	NAME	Editing has no effect on a NAME.
LIKELY USES	To correct mistakes you have made, or to bring your worksheet up to date, with a minimum of effort.	
REFERENCES	Editing, page 59. Word in Quick Reference Guide, page 230.	
ADVICE	Make sure you learn how to use EDIT since it will save you a lot of time.	

HOW TO USE IT	Command	EDIT

TO SELECT THIS COMMAND: either   Press E or e.

or   Press space bar (and backspace) until the
         Command Cursor is over the word 'Edit' and
         then press 'Return'.

THE COMMAND MENU:

    COMMAND LINE   EDIT:

    MESSAGE LINE   Enter a formula.

    This means: The Command Line shows you the formula in the
active cell, if there is one, and the value or text if there
is no formula. This is what you will be using the special
edit keys to alter.

PROPOSED RESPONSE

There is no proposed response for edit, but if you just
press 'Return' the existing value, text or formula will
remain.

EDITING KEYS

You have special keys available for editing. The actual
identity of the keys will depend on your make of
computer. The keys *either* move the Edit Cursor along
the characters or words to be changed, highlighting
them as it does so, *or* delete what the Edit Cursor is
pointing at. There is no key for inserting: you key in
new characters where the Edit Cursor is pointing. This
is how you will use the editing keys:

    CHARACTER   Moves the Edit Cursor one character to the left and
    LEFT   highlights the next **character** to the left of where the
Edit Cursor was before you pressed this key.

    CHARACTER   Moves the Edit Cursor one character to the right and
    RIGHT   highlights the next **character** to the right of where the
Edit Cursor was before you pressed this key.

    WORD LEFT   Moves the Edit Cursor one word to the left and
highlights the next **word** to the left of where the Edit
Cursor was before you pressed this key.

    WORD RIGHT   Moves the Edit Cursor one word to the right and
highlights the next **word** to the right of where the Edit
Cursor was before you pressed this key.

    DELETE   Deletes the word or character that is being highlighted
by the Edit Cursor.

COMPLETION

You may go on editing the contents of the Command
Line until you are satisfied with it. When you have
finished editing it accept it by pressing 'Return'.

WHAT IT DOES   EXTENDED ENTRY

PURPOSE   To speed up the process of entering text and numbers.

RESULTS   Text and numbers are entered in exactly the same way
                                         as with the ALPHA and VALUE commands.

CONTENTS	Previous contents replaced by new text or number.
FORMAT	No change to existing format but text or number will conform to alignment and format code.
FORMULA	Any formula in the cell is lost.
LOCKING	You cannot enter text or values into cells that are locked.
NAME	Entering text or values causes no change to the name.

LIKELY USES   You would use it if you have a lot of data to enter into
                                         the worksheet, for instance, when you enter all this
                                         week's sales figures.

REFERENCES   ALPHA, page 116.

                                         VALUE, page 192.

WARNINGS   If the items that you are entering include numbers that
                                         need to be treated like text (such as a date) then you
                                         cannot do this by using Extended Entry. You must
                                         select the ALPHA command in order to enter them.

ADVICE   Make use of this useful feature: it will save a lot of
                                         time when keying in large volumes of data.

HOW TO USE IT   EXTENDED ENTRY

TO SELECT THIS:

After entering *either* ALPHA *or* VALUE you do not press 'Return' but press a direction key instead.

THE COMMAND MENU:

COMMAND LINE   ALPHA/VALUE:

MESSAGE LINE   Enter text or value.

This means: You may enter text or numbers into the active cell.

PROPOSED RESPONSE   There is no proposed response. The computer is waiting for you to enter the next item of information.

HOW IT WORKS   After each textual or numeric entry you move the arrow keys (up, down, left, right) or the page keys (also up, down, left or right) to the next cell into which you intend to enter. You may repeat the process as often as you like. You may move the direction keys as often as you like between entries.

COMPLETION   When you have finished entering you may exit from Extended Entry mode in one of two ways:

either   Press 'Return' after the last entry.

or   Press the 'Cancel' key.

Both methods will now cause the 20 Commands to appear in the Command Lines and you are back to the main Multiplan menu.

WHAT IT DOES   Command   FORMAT

PURPOSE

To alter the way in which the worksheet displays its information.

RESULTS

The effect of a FORMAT command will be that the information in the worksheet may well look different, although they will remain the same inside the computer.

CONTENTS	All the contents of the selected cells remain unchanged although they may appear to look different.
FORMAT	This is what you are changing with this command.
FORMULA	Any formulas in the selected cells remain unchanged.
LOCKING	Locked cells may not have their FORMATs changed.
NAME	No change.

LIKELY USES

You would use it to improve the readability of the worksheet.

REFERENCES

Formatting, page 60.
Accuracy, page 43.

WARNINGS

A common problem with Multiplan users is that they forget that the FORMAT command does *not* change the way the information is held by the computer. This often leads to an apparent inability to produce the correct answer. Use of mathematical functions, like ROUND and INTEGER are often what is needed to produce the correct degree of accuracy.

ADVICE

Read carefully the special section on formats starting on page 60 since this is a subject that cannot be adequately covered in this way in the Full Reference Guide.

HOW TO USE IT	Command	FORMAT

TO SELECT THIS COMMAND:

either	Press F or f.
or	Press space bar (and backspace) until the Command Cursor is over the word 'Format' and then press 'Return'.

THE COMMAND MENU:

COMMAND LINE	FORMAT: Cells Default Options Width
MESSAGE LINE	Select option or type command letter.
This means:	You must choose which of the four sub-commands the type of FORMATting you need.

THE FOUR SUB-COMMANDS

The difference between the four FORMAT sub-commands is given below. It also tells you which apply to the *whole* of the worksheet and which apply only to a *part*.

PART	FORMAT CELLS will set the alignment and the format codes of the cells that you select in that sub-command.
WHOLE	FORMAT DEFAULT takes you into further options allowing you to specify whether you want to give default formats for all the cells or all the column widths—except where individual formats or column widths have already been set.
WHOLE	FORMAT OPTIONS will let you decide whether to insert commas in numbers and whether to display formulas rather than their results.
PART	FORMAT WIDTH lets you set the column width of an individual column or columns.

PROPOSED RESPONSE

To FORMAT CELLS, just press 'Return'. This will often be what you want to do.

OTHER RESPONSES

You may select the correct sub-command by ONE of the following methods:

either	Press C (or c) or D (or d) or O (or o) or W (or w).
or	Press space bar (and backspace) until the Command Cursor is over the required word, 'Cell' or 'Default' or 'Options' or 'Width'. Then press 'Return'.

THE NEXT STEP

You are now presented with the sub-menu which relates to the sub-command which you have chosen. Each is explained in the following pages.

HOW TO USE IT	**Sub-command**	**FORMAT CELLS**

THE SUB-MENU:

COMMAND LINE

Format Cells: ▓▓▓▓▓▓
alignment: Def Ctr Gen Left Right —
format code: Def Cont Exp Fix Gen Int $ * % —
# of decimals: ▓▓▓▓▓▓

MESSAGE LINE

Enter reference to cell or group of cells.

This means:

You may format a cell or a group of cells.

PROPOSED RESPONSE

The reference on your screen against "Cells:" will be the reference of the active cell. The options in the next three fields will be the current setting of the active cell. You can see which the first two are because they will appear in parentheses. The last will be a number or zero.

You would not accept the proposed response without modification since it would simply reset the format codes of the active cell.

OTHER RESPONSES

You may use the entries in the four fields in this sub-menu to format the specified area.

THE FOUR FIELDS

In each of these four fields you will be *either* accepting the response already there by 'tabbing' on to the next field, *or* entering a response of your own. As soon as you see a set of four correct responses you can leave the command by pressing the 'Return' key.

FIRST FIELD

cells:

Either accept the reference in the first field *or* edit it *or* enter the reference to the cell or cells that you wish to format.

SECOND FIELD

alignment:

Either accept the alignment already highlighted *or* move by using the space bar (and backspace) *or* press the letter or symbol to reach the required choice.

THIRD FIELD

format code:

Either accept the format already highlighted *or* move by using the space bar (and backspace) *or* press the letter or symbol to reach the required choice.

FOURTH FIELD

# of decimals:

Enter the number of decimal places where relevant. (Only with a Format Code of Fix, Exp or %).

COMPLETION

When all four fields are correct you accept them by pressing 'Return'.

| **HOW TO USE IT** | **Sub-command** | **FORMAT DEFAULT** |

THE SUB-COMMAND MENU:

COMMAND LINE   FORMAT DEFAULT: Cells Width.

MESSAGE LINE   Select Option or type command letter.

This means: You can choose from the two sub-commands whether to set the format default settings of cells or column widths.

PROPOSED RESPONSE   The Command Cursor is pointing at 'Cells'. Press 'Return' to set default format settings of cells.

OTHER RESPONSES   You may select the correct sub-command by *one* of the following methods:

either   Press C (or c) or W (or w).

or   Press space bar (and backspace) until the Command Cursor is over the required word, 'Cells' or 'Width'. Then press 'Return'.

THE NEXT STEP   You are now presented with the sub-menu which relates to the sub-command which you have chosen. Each is explained in the following pages.

FULL REFERENCE GUIDE

HOW TO USE IT	Sub-command FORMAT DEFAULT CELLS

THE SUB-MENU:

COMMAND LINE	FORMAT DEFAULT CELLS alignment: Ctr Gen Left Right format code: Cont Exp Fix Gen Int $ * % # of decimals:
MESSAGE LINE	Select option
This means:	You may set default formats for all the cells in the worksheet.

PROPOSED RESPONSE

Both "alignment:" and "format code:" will be initially set at 'General'. "# of decimals:" will be set at zero. Later they will be what you last made it.

You would not accept the proposed response without modification since it would simply reset the format default codes of the worksheet to their current settings.

OTHER RESPONSES

You may use the entries in the three fields in this sub-menu to give the worksheet new default format settings.

THE THREE FIELDS	In each of these three fields you will be *either* accepting the response already there by 'tabbing' on to the next field, *or* choosing a response of your own. As soon as you see a set of three correct responses you can leave the command by pressing the 'Return' key.

FIRST FIELD	alignment:	*Either* accept the alignment already highlighted *or* move by using the space bar (and backspace) *or* press the letter or symbol to reach the required choice.
SECOND FIELD	format code:	*Either* accept the format already highlighted *or* move by using the space bar (and backspace) *or* press the letter or symbol to reach the required choice.
THIRD FIELD	# of decimals:	Enter the number of decimal places where relevant. (Only with a Format Code of Fix, Exp or %).
COMPLETION		When all three fields are correct you accept them by pressing 'Return'.

HOW TO USE IT   Sub-command   FORMAT DEFAULT WIDTH

THE SUB-MENU:

COMMAND LINE

FORMAT DEFAULT WIDTH column width in
chars: ▓▓▓▓

MESSAGE LINE

Enter a number.

This means:

You may choose how wide the default column width for the whole worksheet is going to be. You may choose any width between 3 and 32 character positions.

PROPOSED RESPONSE

When you start a worksheet the initial default width is 10. Later it is what you last entered.

You would not accept the proposed response without modification since it would simply reset the current format default width.

YOUR RESPONSE

Just enter the new default width for all the columns in the worksheet. You express it as a number of character positions, for example: 8.

COMPLETION

When you have entered a number that is correct you accept it by pressing 'Return'.

EXTRA NOTE

This sub-command will only set the width of the columns that *have not* had their individual width set by FORMAT WIDTH.

HOW TO USE IT	**Sub-command**	**FORMAT OPTIONS**

THE SUB-MENU:

COMMAND LINE   FORMAT OPTIONS commas: Yes No formulas: Yes No

MESSAGE LINE   Select Option or type command letter.

This means: You may choose whether to use commas in numbers and also whether to display formulas. These choices apply to the entire worksheet.

PROPOSED RESPONSE   The present settings for these options are shown by the choice being highlighted or appearing in parentheses.

You would not accept the proposed response without modification since it would simply reset the current format options.

THE TWO FIELDS   In each of these two fields you will be *either* accepting the choice already there by 'tabbing' on to the next field, *or* entering a choice of your own. As soon as you see a set of two correct responses you can leave the command by pressing the 'Return' key.

FIRST FIELD   commas: *Either* press Y (or y) or N (or n) *or* move with the space bar (and backspace) until the Command Cursor is over the required word, 'Yes' or 'No'.

SECOND FIELD   formulas: *Either* press Y (or y) or N (or n) *or* move with the space bar (and backspace) until the Command Cursor is over the required word, 'Yes' or 'No'.

COMPLETION   When both fields are correct you accept them by pressing 'Return'.

EXTRA NOTE   If you have entered a FORMAT OPTIONS sub-command choosing commas and you are still not getting any commas, remember that you only get commas in cells with a Format Code of Int, Fix, % and $.

HOW TO USE IT | Sub-command | FORMAT WIDTH

THE SUB-MENU:

COMMAND LINE	FORMAT WIDTH in chars or d(efault): ▓▓▓▓ column: ▓▓▓▓ through: ▓▓▓▓
MESSAGE LINE	Enter a number or d for default.
This means:	You may choose the width of the specified column or columns. The smallest width allowed is 3 and the widest is 32.

PROPOSED RESPONSE

When you start a worksheet the initial proposed width is 10. Later this may be replaced by whatever you chose. The 'd' is set by FORMAT DEFAULT WIDTH: it is also set to 10 initially.

You would not accept the proposed response without modification since it would simply reset the current column width (though you just might be setting the current column's width to the ones on the right).

OTHER RESPONSES

You may use the entries in the three fields in this sub-menu to set a specified width to a stated column or columns.

THE THREE FIELDS

In each of these three fields you will be *either* accepting the entry already there by 'tabbing' on to the next field, *or* entering an entry of your own *or* editing the entry that is already in the field. As soon as you see a set of three correct responses you can leave the command by pressing the 'Return' key.

FIRST FIELD	width in chars or d(efault):	Enter here *either* the column width as a number *or* the letter 'd' to indicate the current default width.
SECOND FIELD	column:	Enter here the column number of the column (or the beginning of the range of columns) in which you want to change the width.
THIRD FIELD	through:	Enter here the end of the range of columns which will have their width changed. If only one column is being changed the number in the third field will be the same as the second field.
COMPLETION		When all three fields are correct you accept them by pressing 'Return'.

WHAT IT DOES	Command	GOTO

PURPOSE
To move the cell pointer to a different part of the worksheet.

RESULTS

CONTENTS	No change.	
FORMAT	No change.	
FORMULA	No change.	
LOCKING	No change.	
NAME	No change.	

LIKELY USES
To save you time when you want to look at another part of your worksheet where you either want to look or enter new information.

REFERENCES
Naming, page 86.

Windows, page 106.

ADVICE
The GOTO NAME method is recommended in preference to the other two. It will save you a lot of time when you need to move to particular parts of a large worksheet.

GOTO ROW-COL is best avoided since Multiplan does not really require you to memorize the actual row and column numbers.

Going to a window is best achieved by using the NEXT WINDOW function key.

HOW TO USE IT	**Command**	**GOTO**

TO SELECT THIS COMMAND:

either   Press G or g.

or   Press space bar (and backspace) until the Command Cursor is over the word 'Goto' and then press 'Return'.

THE COMMAND MENU:

COMMAND LINE   GOTO: Name Row-Col Window.

MESSAGE LINE   Select Option or type command letter.

This means: You can choose from the three sub-commands the method you wish to use for moving the Cell Pointer.

TYPES OF GOTO

The difference between the three types of GOTO is as follows:

GOTO NAME makes use of a cell or group of cells that have already been NAMEd.

GOTO ROW-COL allows you to specify the exact Row and Column to which you want the Cell Pointer to move.

GOTO WINDOW moves the Cell Pointer to the top left of the Window that you specify.

PROPOSED RESPONSE

The Command Cursor is pointing at 'Name'. Press 'Return' to GOTO NAME.

OTHER RESPONSES

You may select the correct sub-command by *one* of the following methods:

either   Press N (or n) or R (or r) or W (or w).

or   Press space bar (and backspace) until the Command Cursor is over the required word, 'Name' or 'Row-Col' or 'Window'. Then press 'Return'.

THE NEXT STEP

You are now presented with the sub-menu which relates to the sub-command which you have chosen. Each is explained in the following pages.

FULL REFERENCE GUIDE

HOW TO USE IT	**Sub-command**	**GOTO NAME**

THE SUB-MENU:

COMMAND LINE

MESSAGE LINE

This means:

GOTO name:

Enter name.

You must indicate the named cell or group of cells to which the Cell Pointer will go.

PROPOSED RESPONSE

There is no proposed response.

ENTERING NAME

You will indicate the name in one of *two* methods:

FIRST METHOD

Type in the actual name.

SECOND METHOD

Use the direction keys to display in the Message Line each of the names recognized by Multiplan for this worksheet. The names appear in the same sequence that they were set up. You move on to 'Completion' when you are satisfied that the correct name is being displayed.

COMPLETION

When the entered name is as you want it you accept it by pressing 'Return'.

ERROR

If you enter a name that is not recognized by Multiplan (probably through misspelling) you will get a 'beep' sound and you will be returned to the two Command Lines.

WHERE THE GOTO GOES

The chosen name either belongs to a cell or a group of cells.

if cell: The Cell Pointer will move to the selected cell.

if group of cells: The Cell Pointer will move to the top left of the named group of cells.

HOW TO USE IT	**Sub-command**	**GOTO ROW-COL**

THE SUB-MENU:

COMMAND LINE

GOTO row: ▓▓▓▓   column: ▓▓▓▓

MESSAGE LINE

Enter a number.

This means:

You may choose to which row and column numbers you want the Cell Pointer to move.

PROPOSED RESPONSE

The entries that you will see on your screen against the words "row:" and "column:" will be the current position of the Cell Pointer.

You would not accept the proposed response without modification since it would simply have the effect of moving the Cell Pointer to its present position.

OTHER RESPONSES

You may use the entries in the two fields in this sub-menu to enter the correct row and column numbers:

FIRST FIELD

row: *Either* enter the row number of the cell you wish to go to *or* accept the number already displayed for you.

SECOND FIELD

column: *Either* enter the column number of the cell you wish to go to *or* accept the number already displayed for you.

COMPLETION

When both fields are correct you accept them by pressing 'Return'.

HOW TO USE IT	Sub-command	GOTO WINDOW

THE SUB-MENU:

COMMAND LINE

GOTO window number: ▓▓▓▓   row: ▓▓▓▓
column: ▓▓▓▓

MESSAGE LINE

Enter a number.

This means:

You may choose to which window and which row and column numbers you want the Cell Pointer to move.

PROPOSED RESPONSE

The entries that you will see on your screen against "window number:" will be the active window number and against the words "row:" and "column:" you will see the current position of the Cell Pointer.

To move the active cell to the top left of the current screen just press 'Return'. This is useful if you want to place the active cell in the top left corner of the screen. This will also work when there is only one window in the worksheet.

OTHER RESPONSES

You may use the entries in the three fields in this sub-menu to enter the correct window, row and column numbers. As soon as you see a set of three correct responses you can leave the command by pressing the 'Return' key.

FIRST FIELD

window number: Enter here the number of the window to which you want the Cell Pointer to move unless the window number is already correct.

SECOND FIELD

row: *Either* enter the number of the row you wish to go to *or* accept the number already displayed for you.

THIRD FIELD

column: *Either* enter the number of the column you wish to go to *or* accept the number already displayed for you.

COMPLETION

When all three fields are correct you accept them by pressing 'Return;.

FULL REFERENCE GUIDE

This page has been left blank on purpose

WHAT IT DOES	**Command**	**HELP**

PURPOSE

To give you assistance in the use of Multiplan directly from the screen.

RESULTS

The worksheet disappears temporarily and you are taken through one or more 'Help' menus. When you leave the command you are returned to the screen in exactly the same state as it was when you selected this command.

CONTENTS	No change.
FORMAT	No change.
FORMULA	No change.
LOCKING	No change.
NAME	No change.

LIKELY USES

You want assistance direct from the screen during a Multiplan session.

   TYPES OF HELP

There are two ways in which you can be asking for 'Help'.

   FIRST

From the Command Menu: when you return at the end of your Help screens you return to the Command Menu.

   SECOND

While executing a command: when you return from your help screens you will be in exactly the same stage of going through that command as when you went to 'Help'.

ADVICE

Since the help messages take space on your disk they are kept as short as possible. They will become more useful to you as your knowledge of Multiplan increases. (If you have had mathematical training you will be able to relate to this material more quickly.)

A useful feature of the 'Help' command is to be able to enter HELP KEYBOARD which tells you how to use special keys on your computer.

HOW TO USE IT	**Command**	**HELP**

TO SELECT THIS COMMAND: either Press H or h.

or Press space bar (and backspace) until the Command Cursor is over the word 'Help' and then press 'Return'.

or Press the special 'Help' key. (On the IBM PC this is done by pressing both 'Alt' and 'H'.)

THE COMMAND MENU:

COMMAND LINE — HELP: Resume Start Next Previous Applications Commands Editing Formulas Keyboard

MESSAGE LINE — Select Option or type command letter.

This means: You can use the first four options to examine the displayed information provided by the last five options.

TYPES OF HELP — A brief explanation of each option appears below:

Resume — Gets you back to the state of the screen at the moment when you asked for 'Help'. This is the proposed response.

Start — Takes you to the beginning of all the 'Help' information.

Next — Moves you on to the next screen's display.

Previous — Returns you to the last screen's display.

Applications — Tries to suggest what you might look up according to what you want to do.

Commands — Studies all 20 commands in alphabetic order.

Editing — Brief description of editing.

Formulas — Explains formulas and lists functions.

Keyboard — How to find all the special Multiplan keys on your particular computer.

RESPONSES — You may select the correct sub-command by *one* of the following methods:

either Press R (or r), S (or s), N (or n), P (or p), A (or a), C (or c), E (or e), F (or f) or K (or k).

or Press space bar (and backspace) until the Command Cursor is over the required word, 'Resume', 'Start', 'Next', 'Previous', 'Applications', 'Commands', 'Editing', 'Formulas' or 'Keyboard'. Then press 'Return'.

WHAT IT DOES	Command	INSERT

PURPOSE

To insert new cells into the worksheet.

RESULTS

The new cells will appear in the worksheet. Areas adjacent to the one that has moved in will be moved out in the direction of the bottom right corner. Wherever possible Multiplan respects all referencing requirements and recalculates them for the new worksheet.

CONTENTS	The new cells will have no contents.
FORMAT	The new cells will have the default format.
FORMULA	The new cells will have no formulas.
LOCKING	The new cells that are INSERTed will not be automatically locked. You are free to lock them now if you need to.
NAME	The new cells that are INSERTed will not be automatically named. You are free to name them now if you need to.

LIKELY USES

You would use it if you needed to make room for fresh information on the worksheet, such as the introduction of some new discounts.

WARNINGS

Remember that the new cells will move into the positions previously occupied by adjacent cells. These new cells will not have the formats, values and formulas of the cells that were there before. They will have no contents and the default formats.

ADVICE

Remember that you do not have to INSERT whole columns or rows. You can often save yourself trouble if you only INSERT the cells that you really need space for, leaving other areas unchanged.

HOW TO USE IT	**Command**	**INSERT**

TO SELECT THIS COMMAND: either   Press I or i.

                                 or   Press space bar (and backspace) until the Command Cursor is over the word 'Insert' and then press 'Return'.

THE COMMAND MENU:

    COMMAND LINE   INSERT: Row Column.

    MESSAGE LINE   Select Option or type command letter.

    This means: You can choose from the two sub-commands whether to insert rows or columns.

PROPOSED RESPONSE   The Command Cursor is pointing at 'Row'. Press 'Return' to insert rows.

OTHER RESPONSES   You may select the correct sub-command by *one* of the following methods:

                    either   Press R (or r) or C (or c).

                    or   Press space bar (and backspace) until the Command Cursor is over the required word, 'Row' or 'Column'. Then press 'Return'.

THE NEXT STEP   You are now presented with the sub-menu which relates to the sub-command which you have chosen. Each is explained in the following pages.

ILLUSTRATED EXAMPLE   Sub-command   INSERT COLUMN

An example of the way that the INSERT COLUMN sub-command works is illustrated on this page.

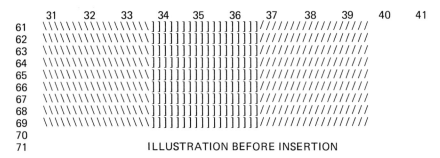

```
      31    32    33    34    35    36    37    38    39    40    41
61  \\\\\\\\\\\\\\\\\]]]]]]]]]]]]]]]]]]/////////////////
62  \\\\\\\\\\\\\\\\\]]]]]]]]]]]]]]]]]]/////////////////
63  \\\\\\\\\\\\\\\\\]]]]]]]]]]]]]]]]]]/////////////////
64  \\\\\\\\\\\\\\\\\]]]]]]]]]]]]]]]]]]/////////////////
65  \\\\\\\\\\\\\\\\\]]]]]]]]]]]]]]]]]]/////////////////
66  \\\\\\\\\\\\\\\\\]]]]]]]]]]]]]]]]]]/////////////////
67  \\\\\\\\\\\\\\\\\]]]]]]]]]]]]]]]]]]/////////////////
68  \\\\\\\\\\\\\\\\\]]]]]]]]]]]]]]]]]]/////////////////
69  \\\\\\\\\\\\\\\\\]]]]]]]]]]]]]]]]]]/////////////////
70
71                 ILLUSTRATION BEFORE INSERTION
```

Suppose that we now select INSERT COLUMN and that the sub-menu fields are entered as follows. The result is shown immediately below.

INSERT COLUMN   # no of columns: 3   starting at: 34
                       between rows: 1 and : 255

```
      31    32    33    34    35    36    37    38    39    40    41
61  \\\\\\\\\\\\\\\\\              ]]]]]]]]]]]]]]]]]]/////////////
62  \\\\\\\\\\\\\\\\\              ]]]]]]]]]]]]]]]]]]/////////////
63  \\\\\\\\\\\\\\\\\              ]]]]]]]]]]]]]]]]]]/////////////
64  \\\\\\\\\\\\\\\\\              ]]]]]]]]]]]]]]]]]]/////////////
65  \\\\\\\\\\\\\\\\\              ]]]]]]]]]]]]]]]]]]/////////////
66  \\\\\\\\\\\\\\\\\              ]]]]]]]]]]]]]]]]]]/////////////
67  \\\\\\\\\\\\\\\\\              ]]]]]]]]]]]]]]]]]]/////////////
68  \\\\\\\\\\\\\\\\\              ]]]]]]]]]]]]]]]]]]/////////////
69  \\\\\\\\\\\\\\\\              ]]]]]]]]]]]]]]]]]]/////////////
70
71           ILLUSTRATION AFTER INSERTING WHOLE COLUMNS
```

But, if the INSERT COLUMN sub-menu selections on the original worksheet had been as follows, then the result would have been:

INSERT COLUMN   # no of columns: 3   starting at: 34
                       between rows: 64 and : 66

```
      31    32    33    34    35    36    37    38    39    40    41
61  \\\\\\\\\\\\\\\\\]]]]]]]]]]]]]]]]]]/////////////////
62  \\\\\\\\\\\\\\\\\]]]]]]]]]]]]]]]]]]/////////////////
63  \\\\\\\\\\\\\\\\\]]]]]]]]]]]]]]]]]]/////////////////
64  \\\\\\\\\\\\\\\\\              ]]]]]]]]]]]]]]]]]]/////////////
65  \\\\\\\\\\\\\\\\\              ]]]]]]]]]]]]]]]]]]/////////////
66  \\\\\\\\\\\\\\\\\              ]]]]]]]]]]]]]]]]]]/////////////
67  \\\\\\\\\\\\\\\\\]]]]]]]]]]]]]]]]]]/////////////////
68  \\\\\\\\\\\\\\\\\]]]]]]]]]]]]]]]]]]/////////////////
69  \\\\\\\\\\\\\\\\\]]]]]]]]]]]]]]]]]]/////////////////
70
71           ILLUSTRATION AFTER INSERTING PART OF COLUMNS
```

HOW TO USE IT   Sub-command   INSERT COLUMN

THE SUB-MENU:

    COMMAND LINE

INSERT COLUMN # of columns: 1 starting at:
between rows: 1 and : 255

    MESSAGE LINE

Enter a number.

    This means:

You may choose where to insert columns, and whether to include whole or partial columns.

PROPOSED RESPONSE

The "starting at:" field on your screen will state the column number where your cell pointer is placed at the moment.

To INSERT a Column just before the one on which the Cell Pointer is placed, just press 'Return'. This will often be what you want to do.

OTHER RESPONSES

You may use the entries in the four fields in this sub-menu to INSERT:

either   One or more than one column.

or   Part of a column or more than one column.

See the illustration on the page opposite.

    THE FOUR FIELDS

In each of these four fields you will be *either* accepting the number already there by 'tabbing' on to the next field, *or* entering a number of your own. As soon as you see a set of four correct responses you can leave the command by pressing the 'Return' key.

    FIRST FIELD

# of columns: Enter the number of columns you wish to insert unless 1 is correct.

    SECOND FIELD

Starting at: Enter the number of the first column you wish to insert unless the correct column number is present.

    THIRD FIELD

between rows: Enter the first row number of the columns you wish to insert unless 1 is correct.

    FOURTH FIELD

and: Enter the last row number of the columns you wish to insert unless 255 is correct.

    COMPLETION

When all four fields are correct you accept them by pressing 'Return'.

ILLUSTRATED EXAMPLE   **Sub-command**   **INSERT ROW**

An example of the way that the INSERT ROW sub-command works is illustrated on this page.

```
      1      2      3      4      5      6      7      8      9      10
 1   \\\\\\\\\\\\\\\\\\\\\\\\\\\\\\\\\\\\\\\\\\\\\\\\\\\\\\\\\\\\\\
 2   \\\\\\\\\\\\\\\\\\\\\\\\\\\\\\\\\\\\\\\\\\\\\\\\\\\\\\\\\\\\\\
 3   \\\\\\\\\\\\\\\\\\\\\\\\\\\\\\\\\\\\\\\\\\\\\\\\\\\\\\\\\\\\\\
 4   ] ] ] ] ] ] ] ] ] ] ] ] ] ] ] ] ] ] ] ] ] ] ] ] ] ] ] ] ] ] ] ]
 5   ] ] ] ] ] ] ] ] ] ] ] ] ] ] ] ] ] ] ] ] ] ] ] ] ] ] ] ] ] ] ] ]
 6   ] ] ] ] ] ] ] ] ] ] ] ] ] ] ] ] ] ] ] ] ] ] ] ] ] ] ] ] ] ] ] ]
 7   //////////////////////////////////////////////////////
 8   //////////////////////////////////////////////////////
 9   //////////////////////////////////////////////////////
10
11                    ILLUSTRATION BEFORE INSERTION
```

Suppose that we now select DELETE ROW and that the sub-menu fields are entered as follows. The result is shown immediately below.

DELETE ROW   # no of rows: 3   starting at: 4
              between columns: 1 and : 63

```
      1      2      3      4      5      6      7      8      9      10
 1   \\\\\\\\\\\\\\\\\\\\\\\\\\\\\\\\\\\\\\\\\\\\\\\\\\\\\\\\\\\\\\
 2   \\\\\\\\\\\\\\\\\\\\\\\\\\\\\\\\\\\\\\\\\\\\\\\\\\\\\\\\\\\\\\
 3   \\\\\\\\\\\\\\\\\\\\\\\\\\\\\\\\\\\\\\\\\\\\\\\\\\\\\\\\\\\\\\
 4
 5
 6
 7   ] ] ] ] ] ] ] ] ] ] ] ] ] ] ] ] ] ] ] ] ] ] ] ] ] ] ] ] ] ] ] ]
 8   ] ] ] ] ] ] ] ] ] ] ] ] ] ] ] ] ] ] ] ] ] ] ] ] ] ] ] ] ] ] ] ]
 9   ] ] ] ] ] ] ] ] ] ] ] ] ] ] ] ] ] ] ] ] ] ] ] ] ] ] ] ] ] ] ] ]
10   //////////////////////////////////////////////////////
11              ILLUSTRATION AFTER INSERTING WHOLE ROWS
```

But, if the INSERT ROW sub-menu selections on the original worksheet had been as follows, then the result would have been:

DELETE ROW   # no of rows: 3   starting at: 4
              between columns: 3 and : 7

```
      1      2      3      4      5      6      7      8      9      10
 1   \\\\\\\\\\\\\\\\\\\\\\\\\\\\\\\\\\\\\\\\\\\\\\\\\\\\\\\\\\\\\\
 2   \\\\\\\\\\\\\\\\\\\\\\\\\\\\\\\\\\\\\\\\\\\\\\\\\\\\\\\\\\\\\\
 3   \\\\\\\\\\\\\\\\\\\\\\\\\\\\\\\\\\\\\\\\\\\\\\\\\\\\\\\\\\\\\\
 4   ] ] ] ] ] ] ] ]                                ] ] ] ] ] ] ] ] ]
 5   ] ] ] ] ] ] ] ]                                ] ] ] ] ] ] ] ] ]
 6   ] ] ] ] ] ] ] ]                                ] ] ] ] ] ] ] ] ]
 7   //////////  ] ] ] ] ] ] ] ] ] ] ] ] ] ] ] ] ] ] ] //////////
 8   //////////  ] ] ] ] ] ] ] ] ] ] ] ] ] ] ] ] ] ] ] //////////
 9   //////////  ] ] ] ] ] ] ] ] ] ] ] ] ] ] ] ] ] ] ] //////////
10               ///////////////////////////////////
11              ILLUSTRATION AFTER DELETING PART OF ROWS
```

HOW TO USE IT	**Sub-command**	**INSERT ROW**

THE SUB-MENU:

COMMAND LINE

INSERT ROW # of rows: 1 starting at: ▮▮▮▮▮
between columns: 1 and : 63

MESSAGE LINE

Enter a number.

This means:

You may choose where to insert rows, and whether to include whole or partial rows.

PROPOSED RESPONSE

The "starting at:" field on your screen will display the row number where your cell pointer is placed at the moment.

To INSERT a row just above the row on which the Cell Pointer is placed, just press 'Return'. This will often be what you want to do.

OTHER RESPONSES

You may use the entries in the four fields in this sub-menu to INSERT:

either   One or more than one row.

or   Part of a row or more than one row.

See the illustration on the page opposite.

THE FOUR FIELDS

In each of these four fields you will be *either* accepting the number already there by 'tabbing' on to the next field, *or* entering a number of your own. As soon as you see a set of four correct responses you can leave the command by pressing the 'Return' key.

FIRST FIELD

# of rows: Enter the number of rows you wish to insert unless 1 is correct.

SECOND FIELD

starting at: Enter the number of the first row you wish to insert unless the correct row number is present.

THIRD FIELD

between columns: Enter the first column of the rows you wish to insert unless 1 is correct.

FOURTH FIELD

and: Enter the last column number of the rows you wish to insert unless 63 is correct.

COMPLETION

When all four fields are correct you accept them by pressing 'Return'.

WHAT IT DOES	**Command**	**LOCK**

PURPOSE

To protect the part of the worksheet that you specify from unauthorized alteration.

RESULTS

CONTENTS	The contents of locked cells will remain unaltered while they are locked.
FORMAT	No change.
FORMULA	You may lock formulas as well as values.
LOCKING	This is the command with which you lock cells or formulas.
NAME	No change.

LIKELY USES

Useful when you build up the worksheet yourself and get someone else to key in the transactions. You will feel safer from accidental loss of permanent data and formulas.

Also useful when moving from one accounting period to the next.

THE TWO USES

Lock is used in two different ways. The status of each type can be switched from Locked to Unlocked, and from Unlocked to Locked, by means of this Command.

CELLS

Locking Cells prevents anyone altering the contents of the Cells that have been locked.

FORMULAS

Locking Formulas has the effect that all the cells in the worksheet containing text or formulas will be protected from change.

REFERENCES

Setting Up a Routine Operation, page 99.

ADVICE

Consider the use of the LOCK FORMULAS sub-command when BLANKing an area in last month's transactions before entering the transactions of this month. This is much more convenient than a set of DELETE commands, which will then have to be followed by FORMATs and setting up of new formulas.

HOW TO USE IT   **Command**   **LOCK**

TO SELECT THIS COMMAND: either   Press L or l.

                                   or   Press space bar (and backspace) until the
                                             Command Cursor is over the word 'Lock' and
                                             then press 'Return'.

THE COMMAND MENU:

    COMMAND LINE   LOCK: Cells Formulas

    MESSAGE LINE   Select option or type command letter.

    This means: You can control the locking of cells *or* formulas.

PROPOSED RESPONSE   The Command Cursor is pointing at cells. Press
                                   'Return' to control the locking of cells.

THE TWO SUB-COMMANDS   The difference between the two sub-commands, from
                                   which you must choose, is explained on the page
                                   opposite.

OTHER RESPONSES   You may select the correct sub-command by *one* of
                                   the following methods:

                                   either   Press C (or c) or F (or f).

                                   or   Press space bar (and backspace) until the
                                             Command Cursor is over the required word,
                                             'Cells' or 'Formulas'. Then press 'Return'.

THE NEXT STEP   You are now presented with the sub-menu which
                                   relates to the sub-command which you have chosen.
                                   Each is explained in the following pages.

HOW TO USE IT	Sub-command	LOCK CELLS

THE SUB-MENU:

COMMAND LINE

LOCK cells: ▓▓▓▓ status: Locked Unlocked.

MESSAGE LINE

Enter a number.

This means:

You will specify which cell or group of cells you wish to control and whether to lock or unlock them.

PROPOSED RESPONSE

On your screen you will see the reference of the active cell and its present locked/unlocked status because one of these two words will be within parentheses.

You would not accept the proposed response without modification since it would simply have the effect of restoring the active cell to its present locking status.

OTHER RESPONSES

You may use the entries in the two fields in this sub-menu to control:

first: The cell or group of cells to be controlled.

second: Whether you are locking or unlocking.

FIRST FIELD

cell or group of cells:

Either enter the reference *or* edit the reference already there. It may be a Relative or Absolute Reference or a Name.

SECOND FIELD

Locked Unlocked:

Choose the new status by *either* pressing L (or l) or U (or u) *or* pressing the space bar (and backspace) until the Command Cursor is over the word 'Locked' or 'Unlocked'.

COMPLETION

When both fields are correct you accept them by pressing 'Return'.

UNLOCKING CELLS

Because the 'Locked/Unlocked' status works on a 'Yes/No' basis you use the same sequence for unlocking cells, just entering 'Unlocked' instead of 'Locked'.

HOW TO USE IT   **Sub-command**   **LOCK FORMULAS**

THE SUB-MENU:

COMMAND LINE

LOCK FORMULAS:

MESSAGE LINE

Enter Y to confirm.

This means:

If you confirm by pressing Y you will lock all the cells containing text and formulas.

PROPOSED RESPONSE

You can only press Y (or y) if you want to lock formulas. (Note that you do *not* see the locked/unlocked status of the LOCK FORMULAS sub-command.)

OTHER RESPONSE

Pressing any other key will have the effect of cancelling LOCK FORMULAS and returning you to the Command Menu.

COMPLETION

Completion is performed for you by adopting either response.

UNLOCKING FORMULAS

To unlock formulas you must use the LOCK CELLS sub-command. There you must choose the cells whose formulas you want to unlock, and choose 'Unlocked' for them.

WHAT IT DOES	Command	MOVE

PURPOSE

To change the position on the worksheet of the specified rows or columns.

RESULTS

The specified rows or columns will be moved to another part of the worksheet, causing a general rearrangement of cells and references. Wherever possible Multiplan respects all referencing requirements and recalculates them for the new worksheet.

CONTENTS	No change.
FORMAT	No change.
FORMULA	Usually no problem: there *could* be a difficulty if MOVE has disturbed a range.
LOCKING	Locked cells may be MOVEd.
NAME	Names are unaffected.

LIKELY USES

You would use it if you needed to rearrange your worksheet.

WARNINGS

Consider carefully before you decide on a MOVE command whether the areas in question contain formulas that make use of relative referencing, which the MOVE command disturbs.

Make sure that you do not move a group of rows or columns onto themselves. Undesirable things tend to happen when you try to do this.

ADVICE

Remember that you cannot MOVE parts of rows or columns.

HOW TO USE IT	Command	MOVE

TO SELECT THIS COMMAND:

either   Press M or m.

or   Press space bar (and backspace) until the Command Cursor is over the word 'Move' and then press 'Return'.

THE COMMAND MENU:

COMMAND LINE   MOVE: Row Column.

MESSAGE LINE   Select Option or type command letter.

This means: You can choose from the two sub-commands whether to move rows or columns.

PROPOSED RESPONSE   The Command Cursor is pointing at 'Row'. Press 'Return' to move rows.

OTHER RESPONSES   You may select the correct sub-command by *one* of the following methods:

either   Press R (or r) or C (or c).

or   Press space bar (and backspace) until the Command Cursor is over the required word, 'Row' or 'Column'. Then press 'Return'.

THE NEXT STEP   You are now presented with the sub-menu which relates to the sub-command which you have chosen. Each is explained in the following pages.

FULL REFERENCE GUIDE

ILLUSTRATED EXAMPLE   Sub-command   MOVE COLUMN

An example of the way that the MOVE COLUMN sub-command works is illustrated on this page.

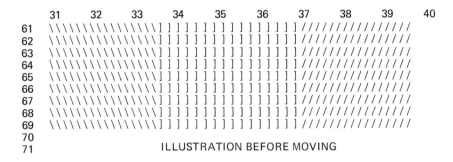

ILLUSTRATION BEFORE MOVING

Suppose that we now select MOVE COLUMN and that the sub-menu fields are entered as follows. The result is shown immediately below.

MOVE COLUMN   from column: 37 to the left of column 34
                # of columns: 3

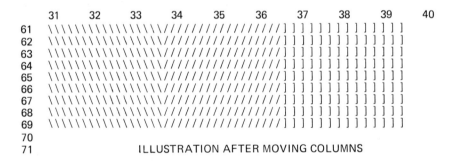

ILLUSTRATION AFTER MOVING COLUMNS

HOW TO USE IT   **Sub-command**   **MOVE COLUMN**

THE SUB-MENU:

COMMAND LINE

MOVE COLUMN from column: ▓▓▓▓
to the left of column: ▓▓▓▓
# of columns: 1

MESSAGE LINE

Enter a number.

This means:

You may choose which columns to MOVE, where to, and how many columns to include in the move.

PROPOSED RESPONSE

The "from column:" field on your screen will display the column number where your cell pointer is placed at the moment. The "# of columns:" field has a 1.

You cannot accept the proposed response without modification since the "to the left of column:" contains no proposed response.

OTHER RESPONSES

You may use the entries in the three fields in this sub-menu to MOVE one or more than one column to a specified position on the worksheet.

See the illustration on the page opposite.

THE THREE FIELDS

In each of these three fields you will be *either* accepting the number already there by 'tabbing' on to the next field, *or* entering a number of your own. As soon as you see a set of three correct responses you can leave the command by pressing the 'Return' key.

FIRST FIELD

from column: Enter the number of the first column you wish to move unless the correct column number is present.

SECOND FIELD

to the left   Enter the number of the column to
of column: the left of which you wish the MOVE
                      to take place.

THIRD FIELD

# of columns: Enter the number of columns you wish to move unless 1 is correct.

COMPLETION

When all three fields are correct you accept them by pressing 'Return'.

ILLUSTRATED EXAMPLE   Sub-command   MOVE ROW

An example of the way that the MOVE ROW sub-command works is illustrated on this page.

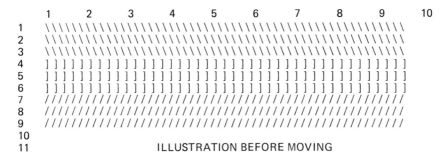

ILLUSTRATION BEFORE MOVING

Suppose that we now select DELETE ROW and that the sub-menu fields are entered as follows. The result is shown immediately below.

MOVE ROW   from row: 7   to before row: 4
            # of rows: 3

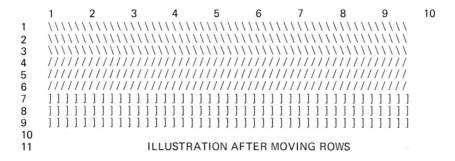

ILLUSTRATION AFTER MOVING ROWS

HOW TO USE IT

Sub-command

MOVE ROW

THE SUB-MENU:

COMMAND LINE

MOVE ROW from row: ▓▓▓▓
to before row: ▓▓▓▓
# of rows: 1.

MESSAGE LINE

Enter a number.

This means:

You may choose which rows to MOVE, where to, and how many rows to include in the move.

PROPOSED RESPONSE

The "from row:" field on your screen will display the row number where your cell pointer is placed at the moment. The "# of rows:" field has a 1.

You cannot accept the proposed response without modification since the "to before row:" field contains no proposed response.

OTHER RESPONSES

You may use the entries in the three fields in this sub-menu to MOVE one or more than one row to a specified position on the worksheet.

See the illustration on the page opposite.

THE THREE FIELDS

In each of these three fields you will be *either* accepting the number already there by 'tabbing' on to the next field, *or* entering a number of your own. As soon as you see a set of three correct responses you can leave the command by pressing the 'Return' key.

FIRST FIELD

from row:

Enter the number of the first row you wish to move unless the correct row number is present.

SECOND FIELD

to before row:

Enter the number of the row above the one to which you wish the MOVE to take place.

THIRD FIELD

# of rows:

Enter the number of rows you wish to move unless 1 is correct.

COMPLETION

When all three fields are correct you accept them by pressing 'Return'.

WHAT IT DOES	**Command**	**NAME**

PURPOSE

To enable you to give names to cells or groups of cells which you can use later on. Also to delete names that you have previously entered.

RESULTS

CONTENTS	Contents are neither affected when you give the area a name nor when you delete the name.
FORMAT	No change.
FORMULA	Formula is neither affected when you give the area a name nor when you delete the name.
LOCKING	You can NAME cells that are locked.
NAME	This is what the command does.

LIKELY USES

You would use NAME for three different purposes:

FIRST

Identifying anywhere in the worksheet instead of using a Relative or an Absolute Reference. The advantage is that it makes it easy to understand what you have done. It's especially useful when you use names in formulas.

SECOND

Letting you move quickly, using GOTO NAME, to another part of the worksheet entering a name which you can easily remember.

THIRD

Helping you to connect worksheets through the eXTERNAL COPY sub-command.

REFERENCES

Naming, page 86.

ADVICE

The third reason above makes a lot of sense if you are using eXTERNAL COPY. The first two make more sense the larger your worksheet is; the smaller it is the less likely that you are going to get advantage out of using NAME.

A major analysis of the use of the NAME command begins on page 86.

Don't forget that you may review all the names on your worksheet by using the 'Reference' key together with your direction keys.

HOW TO USE IT	**Command**	**NAME**

TO SELECT THIS COMMAND: either Press N or n.

or Press space bar (and backspace) until the Command Cursor is over the word 'Name' and then press 'Return'.

THE COMMAND MENU:

COMMAND LINE Name define name: ▓▓▓▓ to refer to: ▓▓▓▓

MESSAGE LINE Enter name.

This means: You can give a name for any cell or group of cells.

PROPOSED RESPONSE On your screen against "define name:" you will see the contents of the active cell (if it begins with a letter). Against the "to refer to:" field you will *normally* see the Reference for the Active Cell (and *sometimes* a Vector, if one was used in a previous NAME command).

To give the name of the text contained in the active cell to the area referenced in the "to refer to:" field just press 'Return'.

OTHER RESPONSES You may build up your response using the information already set up in the Command Line.

THE TWO FIELDS In each of these two fields you will be *either* accepting the contents already there by 'tabbing' on to the next field, *or* making an entry of your own *or* editing the entry that is in the field. As soon as you see a set of two correct responses you can leave the command by pressing the 'Return' key.

FIRST FIELD define name: *Either* key in the text of the NAME you wish to give, *or* accept the name already in the field, *or* edit it.

SECOND FIELD to refer to: *Either* accept the cell reference already in this field, *or* edit it, *or* enter a reference of your own. It may be a Relative or An Absolute Reference or even another Name.

COMPLETION When both fields are correct you accept them by pressing 'Return'.

DELETING A NAME Put the same name in "define name:" and a blank in "to refer to:". Then press 'Return'.

WHAT IT DOES	Command	OPTIONS

PURPOSE

To make some choices regarding the worksheet's way of working.

RESULTS

	CONTENTS	The results of calculation could be affected by this command.
	FORMAT	No change.
	FORMULA	You might wish to change your formulas if you wanted to take advantage of this command.
	LOCKING	Has no effect.
	NAME	No change.

LIKELY USES

Will depend on which of the four options you choose.

THE FOUR FIELDS

RECALC

Normally on. When switched off prevents continuous recalculation of the worksheet every time you key something in.

MUTE

Normally off. When switched on enables you to stop the computer from beeping at you when you make a mistake.

ITERATION

Normally off. When switched on enables you to use circular references with the DELTA and INTERCNT functions.

COMPLETION
TEST AT

Used in connection with ITERATION.

REFERENCES

'It takes too long', page 30.
Iteration, page 75.

WARNINGS

ADVICE

Turning RECALC off can save you a lot of time if you have a lot to enter.

ITERATION requires some mathematical knowledge to use it.

MUTE is unlikely to be of interest to you.

EXTRA MESSAGE

At the end of the OPTIONS command you will see a message appearing in the Message Line telling you which version of Multiplan you have and how much Memory it uses. You can always obtain this information by selecting OPTIONS and immediately pressing 'Return'.

HOW TO USE IT	**Command**	**OPTIONS**

TO SELECT THIS COMMAND: either   Press O or o.

                               or   Press space bar (and backspace) until the Command Cursor is over the word 'Options' and then press 'Return'.

THE COMMAND MENU:

   COMMAND LINE

OPTIONS recalc: Yes No mute Yes No iteration Yes No completion test at: █████

   MESSAGE LINE

Select option.

   This means:

You may decide which options you want.

PROPOSED RESPONSE

The first three fields are either highlighted or in parentheses. The "completion test at:" field will be blank unless you had already put an entry there.

You would not accept the proposed response without modification since it would simply repeat the previous settings.

OTHER RESPONSES

You may use the entries in the four fields in this menu to make your selections.

   THE FOUR FIELDS

In each of the first three fields you will be *either* accepting the setting already there by 'tabbing' on to the next field, *or* entering a setting of your own. You may *either* leave the fourth field blank *or* fill it in. As soon as you see a set of four correct responses you can leave the command by pressing the 'Return' key.

   FIRST FIELD

recalc: *Either* press Y (or y) or N (or n) *or* move the space bar (and backspace) until the Command Cursor is over the word 'Yes' or 'No'.

   SECOND FIELD

mute: *Either* press Y (or y) N (or n) *or* move the space bar (and backspace) until the Command Cursor is over the word 'Yes' or 'No'.

   THIRD FIELD

iteration: *Either* press Y (or y) or N (or n) *or* move the space bar (and backspace) until the Command Cursor is over the word 'Yes' or 'No'.

   FOURTH FIELD

completion test at: Enter *either* an Absolute Reference (pointing is possible) *or* a Name *or* leave it blank.

   COMPLETION

When all four fields are correct you accept them by pressing 'Return'.

WHAT IT DOES	**Command**	**PRINT**

PURPOSE To let you get a printout of all or part of your worksheet.

RESULTS Printing has no effect at all on the worksheet's information.

LIKELY USES You would use it whenever you wanted to get a version of your worksheet to pass on to other people.

THE FOUR SUB-COMMANDS

PRINTER When you are satisfied that your Margins and Options are correct, you select the PRINTER sub-command of the PRINT command.

FILE Enables you to produce a disk file version of your printout information.

MARGINS With this you tell the printer where on the page you want your printed results to appear.

OPTIONS Use this sub-command to define what area of the worksheet you want to print, whether to print row and column numbers, and whether to print formulas instead of values.

REFERENCES Printing, page 92.

ADVICE Printing both "row-col" and formulas is useful when you are developing the worksheet and you are unclear about something. It will give you a 'trace' of what is happening.

Remember to save your worksheet if you want to print with the same margins and options in the future. Multiplan 'remembers' these settings and proposes them with the next LOAD.

| **HOW TO USE IT** | **Command** | **PRINT** |

TO SELECT THIS COMMAND: either   Press P or p.

or   Press space bar (and backspace) until the Command Cursor is over the word 'Print' and then press 'Return'.

THE COMMAND MENU:

COMMAND LINE   PRINT: Printer File Margins Options.

MESSAGE LINE   Select option or type command letter.

This means: You must choose which of the four sub-commands of PRINT you want to select.

THE FOUR SUB-COMMANDS   The difference between the four PRINT sub-commands is explained on the page opposite.

PROPOSED RESPONSE   To PRINT to the printer what has been specified by the current settings of the MARGINS and OPTIONS sub-commands just press 'Return'. Once you have set these two sub-command settings correctly this will be what you will want to do.

OTHER RESPONSES   You may select the correct sub-command by *one* of the following methods:

either   Press P (or p) or F (or f) or M (or m) or O (or o).

or   Press space bar (and backspace) until the Command Cursor is over the required word, 'Printer' or 'File' or 'Margins', or 'Options'. Then press 'Return'.

THE NEXT STEP   You are now presented with the sub-menu which relates to the sub-command which you have chosen. Each is explained in the following pages.

HOW TO USE IT	**Sub-command**	**PRINT FILE**

THE SUB-MENU:

COMMAND LINE   PRINT on file: ▓▓▓▓▓

MESSAGE LINE   Enter a file name.

This means: You may choose the file name for the disk version of the printout that you want. The normal rules for file names on your computer apply.

PROPOSED RESPONSE   There is no proposed response for PRINT FILE: you must always supply a name.

YOUR RESPONSE   You key in the file name you have chosen. If you make a mistake you may use the special editing keys up to the time that you press 'Return'.

COMPLETION   When you are satisfied with the file name that you have entered you accept it by pressing 'Return'.

EXTRA MESSAGE   If there is already a file with the same name, an earlier version perhaps, you will get the following extra message on the Message Line:

'Overwriting existing file?'

YOUR EXTRA RESPONSE   You can press Y (or y) to 'print', that is write the print image to disk. If you don't want to overwrite the existing file you may press any key (whether N or not) and you will be returned to the Main Menu.

HOW TO USE IT	**Sub-command**	**PRINT MARGINS**

THE SUB-MENU:

PRINT MARGINS

left: ░░░ top: ░░░ print width: ░░░
print length: ░░░ page length: ░░░

MESSAGE LINE

Enter a number.

This means:

You can now enter the settings which will define exactly where your worksheet will be printed on the paper.

PROPOSED RESPONSE

The settings on your screen will be:

left

5 first time, later what you last saved.

top

6 first time, later what you last saved.

print width

70 first time, later what you last saved.

print length

54 first time, later what you last saved.

page length

66 first time, later what you last saved.

To PRINT where the settings specify, just press 'Return;. This will often be what you want to do.

OTHER RESPONSES

You may use the entries in the five fields in this sub-menu to define the printing information.

THE FIVE FIELDS

In each of these five fields you will be *either* accepting the number already there by 'tabbing' on to the next field, *or* entering a number of your own. As soon as you see a set of five correct responses you can leave the command by pressing the 'Return' key.

FIRST FIELD

left: Enter the number of blank print positions to the *left* of your margin unless the entry is correct.

SECOND FIELD

top: Enter the number of blank lines you want at the *top* of your page unless the entry is correct.

THIRD FIELD

print width: Enter the number of print positions you want *across* your page from the left margin unless the entry is correct.

FOURTH FIELD

print length: Enter the number of lines per page you want *printed* on *down* the page unless the entry is correct.

FIFTH FIELD

page length: Enter the number of lines there are on the paper *down* the page unless the entry is correct.

COMPLETION

When all five fields are correct you accept them by pressing 'Return'. You will then be returned to the main PRINT command, not the main menu, as you have still to cause printing to take place.

| **HOW TO USE IT** | **Sub-command** | **PRINT OPTIONS** |

THE SUB-MENU:

| COMMAND LINE | PRINT OPTIONS: area: ▓▓▓▓ setup: ▓▓▓▓
formulas: Yes No   row-col: Yes No |

| MESSAGE LINE | Enter reference to cell or group of cells. |

| This means: | You may choose what to print and how to print it. |

PROPOSED RESPONSE

The print area field on your screen will be indeterminate. The "setup:", "formulas:" and "row-col:" fields will indicate the setting that you had last time you printed the worksheet.

To PRINT exactly the same area as last time with setup, formulas and row-col unchanged, just press 'Return'. It still is a good idea to check the area before printing!

OTHER RESPONSES

In each of these four fields you will be *either* accepting the contents already there by 'tabbing' on to the next field, *or* entering contents of your own, *or* editing the contents already there. As soon as you see a set of four correct responses you can leave the command by pressing the 'Return' key.

| FIRST FIELD | area: | Enter the area using Relative or Absolute References or a name. |

| SECOND FIELD | setup: | See page 94 for information on the setup for the printer. |

| THIRD FIELD | formulas | *Either* press Y (or y) or N (or n) *or* move the space bar (and backspace) until the Command Cursor is over the word 'Yes' or 'No'. |

| FOURTH FIELD | row-col: | *Either* press Y (or y) or N (or n) *or* move the space bar (and backspace) until the Command Cursor is over the word 'Yes' or 'No'. |

| COMPLETION | | When all four fields are correct you accept them by pressing 'Return'. You will then be returned to the main PRINT command, not the main menu, as you have still to cause printing to take place. |

HOW TO USE IT	Sub-command	PRINT PRINTER

THE SUB-MENU:

COMMAND LINE

PRINT on Printer.

MESSAGE LINE

This means:

Outputs whatever has been specified by the MARGINS and OPTIONS sub-commands to the printer.

YOUR RESPONSE

Provided that you are happy to go ahead and print just press either P (or p) or just press 'Return'. Otherwise press any other key and you will be returned to the two Command Lines waiting for your next Command.

GENERAL

If you have trouble with printing make sure you read about printing on page 92.

WHAT IT DOES	**Command**	**QUIT**

PURPOSE

To abandon the current worksheet, leave Multiplan and go under the control of your computer's Operating System.

RESULTS

The information in your current worksheet is completely lost, unless you saved it previously.

LIKELY USES

You would use it in order to make a 'tidy' exit from your Multiplan session.

WARNINGS

Make sure that you do not QUIT a session without saving your worksheet. A lot of work can be wasted if you don't save the results!

HOW TO USE IT	Command	QUIT

TO SELECT THIS COMMAND: either   Press Q or q.

                                   or   Press space bar (and backspace) until the Command Cursor is over the word 'Quit' and then press 'Return'.

THE COMMAND MENU:

     COMMAND LINE   Quit:

     MESSAGE LINE   Enter Y to confirm.

     This means: You are given the chance to prevent the computer leaving Multiplan and destroying the worksheet.

PROPOSED RESPONSE   If you are happy to quit just press Y (or y).

OTHER RESPONSE   Otherwise any other key will get you back to the Command Lines.

FULL REFERENCE GUIDE

WHAT IT DOES　　　　　**Command**　　　　　　　**SORT**

PURPOSE

To rearrange the sequence of certain rows according to the contents of a specified column.

RESULTS

The entire rows that you specified are sorted into *either* ascending *or* descending sequence. There should be no change to the information in the worksheet, but consider carefully the warnings below.

LIKELY USES

You would use it in order to rearrange the rows to reflect the changes caused by recent transactions. For instance, you first set up the worksheet in the order of sales performance, highest at the top. Recent transactions have made this sequence incorrect. You use SORT to put the sequence right again.

WARNINGS

Since SORT will rearrange the relative positions of the rows consider carefully whether any of your formulas need to be revised. An example of this is if the first row's formula is different to the formulas in the other rows in the range.

Remember, you *can* sort rows on columns but you cannot sort columns by rows. This is something to bear in mind when you are developing the worksheet in the first place and deciding what is going into rows and what into columns.

ADVICE

Make sure that you restrict the sort to those rows only that you need. 1 and 255 are not likely to be the correct responses to the "between rows" and "and" fields!

You are not limited to sorting on only one column, only one column at a time. If you perform a number of SORTs you can build up a relationship, for instance "gross income" order within "department number".

HOW TO USE IT	**Command**	**SORT**

TO SELECT THIS COMMAND: either   Press S or s.

or   Press space bar (and backspace) until the Command Cursor is over the word 'Sort' and then press 'Return'.

THE COMMAND MENU:

COMMAND LINE

SORT by column: ▓▓▓▓ between rows: ▓▓▓▓ and: ▓▓▓▓ order: (>) <

MESSAGE LINE

Enter a number.

This means:

You can choose which column to SORT on, which range of rows will be sorted, and the sorting sequence.

PROPOSED RESPONSE

On your screen the "by column:" entry is the column number where the Cell Pointer is standing at present. "Between rows:" and "and:" contains *either* the last range you used in this session *or* 1 and 255.

If you want an ascending sort on the active column for the range specified by "between rows:" and "and:" then press 'Return'.

OTHER RESPONSES

You may use the entries in the four fields in this sub-menu to control the sort.

THE FOUR FIELDS

In each of the four fields you can *either* accept the contents already there by 'tabbing' on to the next field, *or* enter new contents. As soon as you see a set of four correct responses you can leave the command by pressing the 'Return' key.

FIRST FIELD

by column: Enter the column number unless field contents are correct.

SECOND FIELD

between rows: Enter the first row number in the range to be sorted unless field contents are correct.

THIRD FIELD

and: Enter the last row number in the range to be sorted unless field contents are correct.

FOURTH FIELD

order   Select > for greater than or < for less than *either* by pressing > or < *or* using space bar (and backspace) until the Command Cursor is over '>' or '<'.

COMPLETION

When all four fields are correct you accept them by pressing 'Return'.

WHAT IT DOES	Command	TRANSFER

PURPOSE To perform important tasks which relate to your worksheets.

RESULTS Will depend entirely on which of the six sub-commands you choose.

LIKELY USES You would need to use these commands to manage the worksheet operations.

THE SIX OPTIONS There are six different options available when you select TRANSFER.

LOAD Transfers the named worksheet from the disk into the memory. You cannot use a SAVEd worksheet until you LOAD it.

SAVE Transfers the contents of the current worksheet from the memory to the disk using the name that you have given it.

CLEAR Sets all the contents of the worksheet to a zero or spaces condition. Almost the same as starting a Multiplan session.

DELETE Removes a named worksheet from the disk.

OPTIONS With OPTIONS you select the Multiplan formats for disk transfers and also you choose the disk drive or directory.

The different formats are:

Normal Multiplan mode.

Symbolic, being suitable for the SYLK, or Symbolic Link system.

Other, which lets you read Visicalc worksheets into Multiplan formats.

RENAME With RENAME you change the name of the active worksheet. If there are eXTERNAL links involved, Multiplan will ensure that all the links are transferred to the new name.

REFERENCE Communicating with Other Computer Systems, page 38.

HOW TO USE IT	Command	TRANSFER

TO SELECT THIS COMMAND:

either   Press T or t.

or   Press space bar (and backspace) until the Command Cursor is over the word 'Transfer' and then press 'Return'.

THE COMMAND MENU:

COMMAND LINE   TRANSFER: Load Save Clear Delete Options Rename

MESSAGE LINE   Select option or type command letter.

This means: You can choose one of six sub-commands. On your screen LOAD will be highlighted.

THE SIX SUB-COMMANDS   The difference between the six TRANSFER sub-commands is explained on the page opposite.

PROPOSED RESPONSE   To LOAD a worksheet from the disk just press 'Return'.

OTHER RESPONSES   You may select the correct sub-command by *one* of the following methods:

either   Press L (or l), S (or s), C (or c), D (or d), O (or o), R (or r).

or   Press space bar (and backspace) until the Command Cursor is over the required word, 'Load' or 'Save' or 'Clear' or 'Delete' or 'Options' or 'Rename'. Then press 'Return'.

THE NEXT STEP   You are now presented with the sub-menu which relates to the sub-command which you have chosen. Each is explained in the following pages.

HOW TO USE IT	**Sub-command**	**TRANSFER CLEAR**

THE SUB-MENU:

COMMAND LINE   TRANSFER CLEAR:

MESSAGE LINE   Enter Y to confirm.

This means: You may empty out the whole worksheet of all its
                                information. You are also given the chance to change
                                your mind!

PROPOSED RESPONSE   If you are happy to clear your worksheet just press 'Y'
                                (or 'y').

OTHER RESPONSE   Otherwise any other key will get you back to the
                                Command Lines.

WHAT HAPPENS   TRANSFER CLEAR takes you *almost* to the same
                                situation when you commence a Multiplan session.

                                All the options that you choose remain in force. These
                                are:

                                > Your settings in the OPTIONS command:
                                > iteration, recalc, mute and completion test at.

                                > Your settings in the OPTIONS sub-command in
                                > the FORMAT, PRINT and TRANSFER commands.

                                Otherwise everything in the previous worksheet is lost.
                                All cells are deleted, columns set to default width,
                                other formats set to General, names are deleted,
                                eXTERNAL links are cleared and the worksheet's name
                                is set to TEMP.

HOW TO USE IT   **Sub-command**   **TRANSFER DELETE**

THE SUB-MENU:

COMMAND LINE   TRANSFER DELETE: ▓▓▓▓▓▓

MESSAGE LINE   Enter a filename, or use the direction keys to view the
                            directory.

This means: You may remove a named worksheet from the disk.

PROPOSED RESPONSE   There is no proposed response for this sub-command.

OTHER RESPONSE   You will tell Multiplan the name of the file (or
                            worksheet, for this purpose it means the same) that
                            you want to DELETE. You do it *either* by keying the
                            name *or* by selecting it from a list of names available.

KEYING IN   You key in the name of the file you want to DELETE
                            making sure that you spell it in exactly the correct
                            manner.

SELECTING   You press one of the direction keys (right arrow is
                            recommended). Your screen is now replaced by a list
                            of all the available worksheets, which is known as a
                            directory. You use the arrows to point to the name you
                            want to select for deletion and press 'Return'.

EXTRA MESSAGE   You will now see a new message on the Message
                            Line, depending on whether your name was valid or
                            not.

VALID   For a valid name you get the message:

                                    'Enter Y to confirm'.

                            You respond with a 'Y' if you are happy to delete the
                            named worksheet. You will be returned to the
                            Command Lines your deletion having taken place.
                            Press any other key to get back to the Command Lines
                            without any deleting taking place.

INVALID   If the name you specified is not recognized as one that
                            has been SAVEd you will get a message saying 'Invalid
                            parameter' and you will be returned to the Command
                            Lines.

| **HOW TO USE IT** | **Sub-command** | **TRANSFER LOAD** |

THE SUB-MENU:

COMMAND LINE

TRANSFER LOAD:

MESSAGE LINE

Enter a filename, or use the direction keys to view the directory.

This means:

You may load a named worksheet from the disk for use in a Multiplan session. The "TRANSFER LOAD:" field will appear blank on your screen.

PROPOSED RESPONSE

There is no proposed response for this sub-command.

OTHER RESPONSE

You will tell Multiplan the name of the file (or worksheet, for this purpose it means the same) that you want to LOAD. You do it *either* by keying the name *or* by selecting it from a list of names available.

KEYING IN

You key in the name of the file you want to LOAD making sure that you spell it in exactly the correct manner.

SELECTING

You press one of the direction keys (right arrow is recommended). Your screen is now replaced by a list of all the available worksheets. You use the arrows to point to the name you want to select for loading and press 'Return'.

RESULT

The result will depend on whether you selected a valid name.

VALID

Entering a valid name has the effect of replacing your present worksheet with the selected one. You will also be returned to the Command Lines.

INVALID

If you specified a name that has not been SAVEd you will see a message saying 'Enter Y to retry access to [name of your file]'. If you press Y, then your next message will be 'Cannot read file'. You will then be returned to the Command Lines. During this time you have the opportunity to get the name right. The easiest way of doing this is to use the direction key and point to the correct name. You also have the opportunity to change the diskette if you find that the wrong one is mounted.

WARNING

If you issue this sub-command by mistake, you will have lost the active worksheet. In this case you are *not* given a second chance by being prompted by 'Enter Y to confirm'.

HOW TO USE IT   Sub-command   TRANSFER OPTIONS

THE SUB-MENU:

    COMMAND LINE

TRANSFER OPTIONS: mode: Normal Symbolic Other
setup:

    MESSAGE LINE

Enter the text.

    This means:

You are going to select whether to work in 'normal'
Multiplan mode or one of the others. You may also
organize your worksheets into different groups using
the "setup:" field.

PROPOSED RESPONSE

You will see the "mode:" field highlighted as Normal.
No response is made for setup, unless you have
already made an entry which will then appear here.

To set up the Transfer Options as the Normal
Multiplan mode just press 'Return'.

OTHER RESPONSES

In each of these two fields you will be *either* accepting
the contents already there by 'tabbing' on to the next
field, *or* making an entry of your own, *or* editing the
entry that is in the field. As soon as you see a set of
two correct responses you can leave the command by
pressing the 'Return' key.

    FIRST FIELD

mode: *Either* press the N (or n), S (or s) or O (or o),
or move the space bar (and backspace) until
the Command Cursor is over the word
'Normal' or 'Symbolic' or 'Other' *or* accept
what is already there.

    SECOND FIELD

setup: Select here the default file transfer
commands your operating system will use
in all subsequent TRANSFER commands
until the setup is changed. For example 'B:'
will cause all subsequent LOADs and
SAVEs to take place on drive B. Another
example: if you LOAD '*.JOE' and press the
direction key, you will only see the
worksheets displayed with the filename
.JOE at the end. This lets you split your
worksheets into different categories (known
as sub-directories).

    COMPLETION

When both fields are correct you accept them by
pressing 'Return'.

REFERENCE

For an explanation of 'Normal', 'Symbolic' and 'Other'
see 'Communicating with Other Computer Systems',
page 38.

HOW TO USE IT   Sub-command   **TRANSFER RENAME**

THE SUB-MENU:

    COMMAND LINE   TRANSFER RENAME:

    MESSAGE LINE   Enter a filename.

    This means: You may give the active worksheet a new name.

PROPOSED RESPONSE   You will see the name of the active worksheet on your screen against "TRANSFER RENAME:".

                                    The proposed response would only be of use if you wanted to edit it. Otherwise it only enables you to change the worksheet's name to itself.

OTHER RESPONSE   You will tell Multiplan the name of the file (or worksheet, for this purpose it means the same) that you want to replace the present name with. You do it *either* by keying the name *or* by editing the existing name.

RESULT   The active worksheet is now known to Multiplan by its new name. Any links set up by eXTERNAL COPY will take account of the new name.

HOW TO USE IT	Sub-command	TRANSFER SAVE

THE SUB-MENU:

COMMAND LINE | TRANSFER SAVE: ▨

MESSAGE LINE | Enter a filename.

This means: | You may save the active worksheet onto the disk. You will get the entire worksheet back when you TRANSFER LOAD it. You will get the Cell Pointer back exactly where you have left it.

PROPOSED RESPONSE

The "TRANSFER SAVE:" field on your screen will display the present name, if there is one, otherwise TEMP, meaning 'temporary'.

To save the active worksheet with the name displayed, just press 'Return'.

OTHER RESPONSE

You will tell Multiplan the name of the file (or worksheet, for this purpose it means the same) that you want to SAVE. You do it *either* by keying the name *or* by editing the name that is already there. Then press 'Return'.

COMPLETION

As you complete this command you will see the new name of the worksheet appearing on the right end of the Status Line. The worksheet will remain unaltered on your screen. You will be returned back to the Command Lines.

ADVICE

Do not use this command to change a worksheet's name if it has eXTERNAL links, since the new name will not recognize the links made with the old names. For that purpose you should use TRANSFER RENAME.

It is good practice to leave the Cell Pointer 'Home' every time you TRANSFER SAVE, unless you have set up the worksheet with prompts for a data entry operation.

WHAT IT DOES	Command	VALUE

PURPOSE   To enter a number or a formula into a cell.

RESULTS

	CONTENTS	The old contents will be replaced by the new.
	FORMAT	No change.
	FORMULA	The old formula will be replaced by the new information.
	LOCKING	You cannot enter into a locked cell.
	NAME	No change.

LIKELY USES   You will be entering numbers and formulas into Multiplan worksheets very often.

ADVICE   You do not need to select VALUE from the Command Lines since the following symbols all inform Multiplan that a VALUE Command is being entered:

$$0\ 1\ 2\ 3\ 4\ 5\ 6\ 7\ 8\ 9$$

$$= + - . \,($$

All these symbols are taken as showing that what follows is either a number or a formula.

HOW TO USE IT	Command	VALUE

TO SELECT THIS COMMAND:

either   Press V or v.

or   Press space bar (and backspace) until the Command Cursor is over the word 'Value' and then press 'Return'.

or   Press any one of the following keys to signify the start of a number of formula:

       0 1 2 3 4 5 6 7 8 9

       = + − . (

THE COMMAND MENU:

COMMAND LINE   VALUE: ▨

MESSAGE LINE   Enter a formula.

This means: You may enter *either* a number, *or* a formula. You will see in the "VALUE:" field on the screen the present number, if there is one.

PROPOSED RESPONSE

You would be unlikely to accept the proposed response without alteration since it would simply return the present numerical value into the active cell.

OTHER RESPONSES

You may enter your number or formula according to the rules for doing so.

EXTENDED ENTRY

When you are entering information, whether numeric and/or text, you may speed up the task by going into the Extended Entry mode. You do not have to press 'Return' after each entry if you press a directional key instead. See page 136 for extra information.

WHAT IT DOES	Command	WINDOW

PURPOSE   To let you look at separate areas of your worksheet at the same time.

RESULTS   No change takes place to any part of the worksheet.

LIKELY USES   You would use it whenever you wanted to look at different areas of the worksheet at the same time. For example, you are entering some figures about bonuses and you want to see the total as it builds up.

THE FOUR OPTIONS

    SPLIT   This option takes you into further options allowing you to specify whether you want to split the screen horizontally, vertically or four ways in order to have titles along the top and the side of the screen.

    BORDER   Lets you put a Border around a Window, and lets you close it up again.

    CLOSE   Closes a Window.

    LINK   Lets you link (and unlink) two adjacent windows, if you have not already linked them by using the "link:" field in the WINDOW SPLIT sub-command.

REFERENCES   Windows, page 106.

ADVICE   If you have a large worksheet and you are spending a lot of time moving the Cell Pointer around, you should consider whether to make life simpler by setting up one or more windows.

                You will also be using the special key known as 'Next Window'.

HOW TO USE IT	**Command**	**WINDOW**

TO SELECT THIS COMMAND: either   Press W or w.

or   Press space bar (and backspace) until the Command Cursor is over the word 'Window' and then press 'Return'.

THE COMMAND MENU:

COMMAND LINE   WINDOW: Split Border Close Link.

MESSAGE LINE   Select option or type command letter.

This means: You must choose which of the four sub-commands of WINDOW you want to select.

THE FOUR SUB-COMMANDS   The difference between the four WINDOW sub-commands is explained on the page opposite.

PROPOSED RESPONSE   You will see split highlighted.

To select WINDOW SPLIT just press 'Return'.

OTHER RESPONSES   You may select the correct sub-command by *one* of the following methods:

either   Press S (or s) or B (or b) or C (or c) or L (or l).

or   Press space bar (and backspace) until the Command Cursor is over the required word, 'Split' or 'Border' or 'Close' or 'Link'. Then press 'Return'.

THE NEXT STEP   You are now presented with the sub-menu which relates to the sub-command which you have chosen. Each is explained in the following pages.

HOW TO USE IT	Sub-command	WINDOW BORDER

THE SUB-MENU:

COMMAND LINE

WINDOW change border in window number: ▓▓▓▓

MESSAGE LINE

Enter a number.

This means:

You will use this sub-command to 'draw' a border round a window, or to take it away.

PROPOSED RESPONSE

You will see in the "window number:" field the number of the active window.

If you want to change the border of the active window to its opposite status (on to off, or off to on) just press 'Return'.

OTHER RESPONSES

You can replace the number of the active window with any other valid window number.

COMPLETION

When you are satisfied that you have the correct window number you accept it by pressing 'Return'.

EXTRA NOTE

Borders greatly improve the presentation of the windows because they make it clear what is inside the window and what is not. However, they also take up valuable space on the worksheet. Each border takes up two rows and two column width positions.

REMOVING BORDERS

You remove a border in exactly the same way as you put it there. You simply reverse the 'on/off' status. This is also true when you have a single border around the entire worksheet.

HOW TO USE IT Sub-command WINDOW CLOSE

THE SUB-MENU:

COMMAND LINE

WINDOW close window number: ▓▓▓

MESSAGE LINE

Enter a number.

This means:

You will use this sub-command to remove the window number that has been specified. The remaining windows take up the space made available.

PROPOSED RESPONSE

The screen will display in the "window number:" field the number of the active window.

If you want to close the active window just press 'Return'.

OTHER RESPONSES

You can replace the number of the active window with any other valid window number.

COMPLETION

When you are satisfied that you have the correct window number you accept it by pressing 'Return'.

RESULT

All the window numbers which are greater than the one that you have removed will now be renumbered as one less.

EXTRA NOTE

If you try to close the only window, window #1, this will be ignored. There is always one window in Multiplan.

FULL REFERENCE GUIDE

HOW TO USE IT	**Sub-command**	**WINDOW LINK**

THE SUB-MENU:

COMMAND LINE

WINDOW LINK: window number: ▓▓▓▓
with window number: ▓▓▓▓
linked: Yes No

MESSAGE LINE

Enter a number.

This means:

You will use this sub-command to set up a link between two adjacent windows, so that the information in each will move in harmony as you scroll them across the screen. Also used to undo the link.

PROPOSED RESPONSE

The "window number:" suggested on your screen will be the active window plus an adjacent window. The "linked:" field will display the current linked status.

If you want to link the active window with the displayed "with window number:" just press 'Return'.

OTHER RESPONSES

In each of these three fields you will be *either* accepting the contents already there by 'tabbing' on to the next field, *or* entering contents of your own. As soon as you see a set of three correct responses you can leave the command by pressing the 'Return' key.

FIRST FIELD

window number:

Enter the number of the first window *or* accept the number already there.

SECOND FIELD

with window number:

Enter the number of the second window *or* accept the number already there.

THIRD FIELD

Linked

Either press Y (or y) or N (or n) *or* move the space bar (and backspace) until the Command Cursor is over the word 'Yes' or 'No'.

COMPLETION

When you are satisfied that you have the correct window numbers and "linked:" status you accept them by pressing 'Return'.

RESULT

The linkage has been made or removed as you specified.

ERROR MESSAGE

If you have specified a pair of windows that cannot be linked (or unlinked) you will get a message saying: 'Cannot link those windows'.

REMOVING LINKAGE

You remove a linkage between two windows in the same way, remember to put a 'No' as the entry in the "linked:" field.

HOW TO USE IT   Sub-command   WINDOW SPLIT

THE SUB-MENU:

COMMAND LINE

WINDOW SPLIT: Horizontal Vertical Titles.

MESSAGE LINE

Select option or type command letter.

This means:

You will use this sub-command to open up a new window. This is done by splitting it with the active window, suitable for scrolling sideways, top to bottom and up again, and fixing titles along the top and the left of the worksheet.

PROPOSED RESPONSE

The word 'Horizontal' will be highlighted on your screen.

If you want to split the active window horizontally just press 'Return'.

OTHER RESPONSES

You may select the correct sub-command by *one* of the following methods:

either   Press H (or h) or V (or v) or T (or t).

or   Press space bar (and backspace) until the Command Cursor is over the required word, 'Horizontal' or 'Vertical' or 'Titles'. Then press 'Return'.

THE NEXT STEP

You are now presented with the sub-menu which relates to the sub-command which you have chosen. Each is explained in the following pages.

HOW TO USE IT   Sub-command   WINDOW SPLIT HORIZONTAL

THE SUB-MENU:

COMMAND LINE	WINDOW SPLIT HORIZONTAL at row: ▓▓▓▓▓ linked: Yes No
MESSAGE LINE	Enter a number.
This means:	You will use this sub-command to split the active window horizontally into two parts, one above the other. You will decide on which row number the split is to take place and whether the two parts should be linked to move in harmony with each other.

PROPOSED RESPONSE

Your screen will suggest that the split should be at the active row, and that the two new windows should *not* be linked.

If you want to split the active window horizontally on the active row without linking them just press 'Return'.

OTHER RESPONSES

In each of these two fields you will be *either* accepting the contents already there by 'tabbing' on to the next field, *or* making an entry of your own, *or* editing the entry that is in the field. As soon as you see a set of two correct responses you can leave the command by pressing the 'Return' key.

FIRST FIELD	at row:	*Either* enter a row number *or* accept what is already there.
SECOND FIELD	linked:	*Either* press Y (or y) or N (or n) *or* move the space bar (and backspace) until the Command Cursor is over the word 'Yes' or 'No'.
COMPLETION		When both fields are correct you accept them by pressing 'Return'.

RESULT

The new window is given a window number one greater than the last one open. It now becomes the active window.

The appearance of your screen will differ according to whether you have chosen to make the split linked or not.

UNLINKED

The new window that has been created will repeat the column numbers above the displayed area of the worksheet. This is because, being unlinked, you will need the column numbers when you start scrolling sideways.

LINKED

If the two windows are linked the second window has no separate column numbers as they are not needed. You get more of the worksheet displayed instead.

HOW TO USE IT	Sub-command	WINDOW SPLIT TITLES

THE SUB-MENU:

COMMAND LINE

WINDOW SPLIT TITLES: # of rows:
# of columns:

MESSAGE LINE

Enter a number.

This means:

You will use this sub-command to split the active window both horizontally and vertically so that you can view titles at the top and on the left of the screen.

PROPOSED RESPONSE

The "# of rows:" and "# of columns:" fields (row and column number relative to the top left of the current window) determine how big the windows at the top and on the left are. The bottom right window becomes the active window. The prompts on the screen would have the effect of placing the active cell in the top left corner of the new active window.

If you want to split the active window into four with both horizontal and vertical scrolling possible and with the active cell just below the horizontal titles and just to the right of the vertical titles then just press 'Return'.

OTHER RESPONSES

In each of these two fields you will be *either* accepting the contents already there by 'tabbing' on to the next field, *or* making an entry of your own, *or* editing the entry that is in the field. As soon as you see a set of two correct responses you can leave the command by pressing the 'Return' key.

FIRST FIELD

# of rows: *Either* enter a row number *or* accept what is already there.

SECOND FIELD

# of columns: *Either* enter a column number *or* accept what is already there.

COMPLETION

When both fields are correct you accept them by pressing 'Return'.

RESULT

You can now scroll two ways and the titles remain visible. You are not given the choice of 'linked/unlinked' in this sub-command: WINDOW SPLIT TITLES windows are always linked.

HOW TO USE IT   **Sub-command**   **WINDOW SPLIT VERTICAL**

THE SUB-MENU:

COMMAND LINE   WINDOW SPLIT VERTICAL at column: ▓▓▓▓
                                linked: Yes No

MESSAGE LINE   Enter a number.

This means: You will use this sub-command to split the active
                                window vertically into two parts, one to the right of
                                the other. You will decide on which column number
                                the split is to take place and whether the two parts
                                should be linked to move in harmony with each other.

PROPOSED RESPONSE   Your screen will suggest that the split should be at the
                                active column, and that the two new windows should
                                not be linked.

                                If you want to split the active window vertically on the
                                active column without linking them just press 'Return'.

OTHER RESPONSES   In each of these two fields you will be *either* accepting
                                the contents already there by 'tabbing' on to the next
                                field, *or* making an entry of your own, *or* editing the
                                entry that is in the field. As soon as you see a set of
                                two correct responses you can leave the command by
                                pressing the 'Return' key.

FIRST FIELD   at column: *Either* enter a column number *or* accept
                                             what is already there.

SECOND FIELD   linked: *Either* press Y (or y) or N (or n) *or* move
                                             the space bar (and backspace) until the
                                             Command Cursor is over the word 'Yes'
                                             or 'No'.

COMPLETION   When both fields are correct you accept them by
                                pressing 'Return'.

RESULT   The new window is given a window number one
                                greater than the last one open. It now becomes the
                                active window.

                                The appearance of your screen will differ according to
                                whether you have chosen to make the split linked or
                                not.

UNLINKED   The new window that has been created will repeat the
                                row numbers on the left of the displayed area of the
                                worksheet. This is because, being unlinked, you will
                                need the row numbers when you start scrolling up and
                                down.

LINKED   If the two windows are linked the second window has
                                no separate row numbers as they are not needed. You
                                get more of the worksheet displayed instead.

This page has been left blank on purpose

WHAT IT DOES	Command	eXTERNAL

PURPOSE

To enable you to get information automatically across from one worksheet to another.

RESULTS

The receiving worksheet gets its information from the sending worksheet.

LIKELY USES

You would use it whenever you wanted to associate different sets of data together. You might be building up departmental worksheets, each quite complex. In addition to the departmental worksheets, you might wish to work on a corporate basis taking the figures from the different departments into a summary worksheet. All this, and much more, can be done by using the eXTERNAL command.

THE THREE SUB-COMMANDS

COPY

This sub-command permits you to specify the external worksheet and its data that you wish to have copied into the active worksheet. As a further option you may decide whether to copy it just once, or to make sure that all later changes in the sending worksheet are reflected in the receiving worksheet.

LIST

Lets you list the relationships between supporting and dependent worksheets.

USE

Lets you replace one external worksheet for another so that the effective linkage is altered.

REFERENCES

Connecting Worksheets, page 45.

ADVICE

This is the most powerful command in Multiplan. It will repay careful study.

Consider whether you want to make one large worksheet or several smaller ones that are linked together. A large worksheet will slow you down and will create greater problems if you want to enlarge. Several smaller ones that are linked are usually faster and offer greater flexibility.

HOW TO USE IT	**Command**	**eXTERNAL**

TO SELECT THIS COMMAND:

either   Press X or x.

or   Press space bar (and backspace) until the
         Command Cursor is over the word 'eXternal'
         and then press 'Return'.

THE COMMAND MENU:

COMMAND LINE   XTERNAL: Copy List Use

MESSAGE LINE   Select option or type command letter.

This means: You must choose which of the three sub-commands of
                      eXTERNAL you want to select.

THE THREE SUB-COMMANDS   The difference between the three eXTERNAL sub-
                          commands is explained on the page opposite.

PROPOSED RESPONSE   On your screen you will see the word COPY
                          highlighted.

                          To select eXTERNAL COPY just press 'Return'.

OTHER RESPONSES   You may select the correct sub-command by *one* of
                          the following methods:

                          either   Press C (or c) or L (or l) or U (or u).

                          or   Press space bar (and backspace) until the
                                   Command Cursor is over the required word,
                                   'Copy' or 'List' or 'Use'. Then press 'Return'.

THE NEXT STEP   You are now presented with the sub-menu which
                          relates to the sub-command which you have chosen.
                          Each is explained in the following pages.

HOW TO USE IT   Sub-command   eXTERNAL COPY

THE SUB-MENU:

COMMAND LINE	XTERNAL COPY from sheet: ▨ name: ▨ to: ▨ linked: Yes No

MESSAGE LINE — Enter a name.

This means: You will use this sub-command to specify the sending worksheet, the area in that worksheet, the destination in the active worksheet, and whether there is to be a permanent link.

PROPOSED RESPONSE

The "from sheet:" field will be blank if you have not used this sub-command before, otherwise it will be the last sheet used as a source for an XTERNAL COPY. The "name:" field will be blank; but you can retrieve other names used by using the direction keys. The "to:" field will be the active cell. The "linked:" prompt will be 'Yes'.

You cannot accept the proposed response without modification since it is incomplete.

OTHER RESPONSES

In each of these four fields you will be *either* accepting the contents already there by 'tabbing' on to the next field, *or* making an entry of your own, *or* editing the entry that is in the field. As soon as you see a set of four correct responses you can leave the command by pressing 'Return'.

FIRST FIELD — from sheet: *Either* enter a sheet name *or* accept what is already there.

SECOND FIELD — name: *Either* enter the name of the sending area (or its Absolute Reference) *or* use the arrow key until the correct name is displayed.

THIRD FIELD — to: *Either* enter here the References of the receiving area using Absolute or Relative Referencing or Name *or* accept the Reference that is already there.

FOURTH FIELD — link: *Either* press Y (or y) or N (or n) *or* move the space bar (and backspace) until the Command Cursor is over the word 'Yes' or 'No'.

COMPLETION — When all four fields are correct you accept them by pressing 'Return'.

REMOVING AN EXTERNAL COPY

You remove an external copy in a manner similar to setting it up: repeat everything for setting up *but* the third field, "to:" must be *blank*.

HOW TO USE IT	Sub-command	eXTERNAL COPY
RESULTS	CONTENTS	The contents of the receiving cells will be replaced by the sending cells.
	FORMAT	The format of the receiving cells will be unchanged.
	FORMULA	The formula of the receiving cells will be lost. The formulas of the sending cells will also be lost: you just get the value instead.
	LOCKING	You cannot copy into a locked cell.
	NAME	You may copy from a named area: the receiving area will *not* automatically take the name of the sending area. You *may* name it afterwards.

FULL REFERENCE GUIDE

| **HOW TO USE IT** | **Sub-command** | **eXTERNAL LIST** |

THE SUB-MENU:

COMMAND LINE	Is blank.
MESSAGE LINE	Press any key to redraw screen.
This means:	You will temporarily lose your display of the worksheet and see a list of all linkages that relate to the active worksheet. This will indicate which are supporting, which are depending and which have had eXTERNAL USE applied. Pressing any key returns the previous screen to you.

PROPOSED RESPONSE   No response is required.

HOW TO USE IT **Sub-command** **eXTERNAL USE**

THE SUB-MENU:

COMMAND LINE

XTERNAL USE filename: ▓▓▓
instead of: ▓▓▓

MESSAGE LINE

Enter name.

This means:

You will provide a pair of names of worksheets (called filenames for this purpose). Whatever has been used in eXTERNAL COPY for the first name will now be replaced by the second name.

PROPOSED RESPONSE

The "filename:" field on you screen will be blank. The second, "instead of:", will be blank unless you have used eXTERNAL USE before, in which case it will be the last name used.

You cannot accept the proposed response without modification since it is incomplete.

OTHER RESPONSES

In each of these two fields you will be *either* accepting the contents already there by 'tabbing' on to the next field, *or* making an entry of your own, *or* editing the entry that is in the field. As soon as you see a set of two correct responses you can leave the command by pressing the 'Return' key.

FIRST FIELD

filename: Enter a sheet name.

SECOND FIELD

instead of: *Either* enter a sheet name *or* accept what is already there.

COMPLETION

When both fields are correct you accept them by pressing 'Return'.

PART 4
QUICK
REFERENCE GUIDE

Introduction

The purpose of this Quick Reference Guide is to save you time. If you want to look something up quickly you won't want to search through the various chapters of this book unless you have to. This guide is intended to answer the majority of your quick questions.

All the technical terms used in Multiplan are defined here. Where this Guide makes use of words that are defined somewhere else (whether in the manufacturer's manual, the screen messages or the help commands), this will be made clear to you because they are all printed **bold**. Actual Multiplan commands are indicated by the use of UPPER CASE.

Many words are defined in this Guide at two different levels, identified by a 1 and a 2. Level 1 just tells you what it means, providing you with a Glossary. Level 2 always goes further, trying to anticipate the reason why you went to this Quick Reference Guide. Let's hope it succeeds!

Absolute reference

1.   The method of indicating a **cell**'s position which identifies its row and column position. For instance, R3C8 means the third row of the eighth column.
2.   This is the opposite of **Relative Reference** where the reference is worked out by looking at where the **cell pointer** is at the moment. But this absolute reference also gets renumbered along with everything else that's involved whenever you modify the worksheet by INSERT, DELETE or MOVE. All the Absolute References, and the Relative ones too, get recalculated to what they should be.

Active

1.   What you're using at the moment.
2.   In Multiplan, it has the following different meanings:

active cell: where the **cell pointer** is at the start of a command;
active column: the column in which the **cell pointer** is placed;
active command: the command that you're working on at the moment;
active row: the row in which the **cell pointer** is placed;
active sheet: the worksheet that you are working on at the moment, by contrast to the others that could be linked with it but are on the disk;
active window: the window where the **cell pointer** is placed at the moment.

Alignment

1.   The position of the contents of a cell: on the left, on the right or in the middle. Alignment codes are entered in response to the Alignment Code field of the FORMAT Command.
2.   Remember that this refers only to the appearance of the cell's contents: the computer holds it in its own way. If you need to alter the way the computer holds the information you will have to use a function to do it.

ALPHA/VALUE

The 'Alpha/Value' message appears in the **command line** when you enter a ALPHA or VALUE by an arrow movement instead of pressing 'Enter'. This method of speeding up keyboard operations is called **extended entry**.

Area

This is a convenient word used to describe either a **cell** or a group of cells.

Argument

1.   A mathematical term used in Multiplan in connection with functions.
2.   When you use a **function**, you generally have to supply one or more pieces of information inside **parentheses**. These are known as arguments.

BASIC

1. The name of a programming language.
2. One of the main objectives of Multiplan is that you should not have to know how to program in order to benefit from using computers. Nevertheless for advanced activities Multiplan conforms mainly to the rules of BASIC. This is particularly true of the way that you use the *functions*, but also the way that the rules work, such as the distinction between numbers and **text strings**. In summary, you don't need to know BASIC to use Multiplan, but if you do know it you will be able to learn some features more quickly.

Brackets

The [and] symbols that are used by Multiplan in identifying cells that have been externally copied.

Catenate

1. This means joining together different pieces of **text**.
2. You use it with the & symbol. It is also called **catenation** and you may also say that you will **concatenate** two pieces of text. It only works on text, not on numbers.

Cell

The place where one **row** meets one **column**. Contains a **value**, a **formula** or **text**.

Cell Pointer

The Cell Pointer is used to show where we are making changes in the **display area** of the screen.

Character

The symbol that occupies one position on the screen and on the printed page. It can be a letter, a number or any other symbol such as /, * or @.

Character string

This is a term meaning **text** which is the term used in this book.

Circular reference

1. When one cell gets its value from another which gets its value from the first, that is called a circular reference. For instance, the surcharge is 2.5 per cent of the final total, and the final total includes the surcharge. The chain of references can be much longer than this simple example. Multiplan does not normally try to resolve them. You will get a message on the Message Line saying: 'Circular references unresolved'.

2. The previous example would almost certainly be an error. The 'Circular references unresolved' message usually means that you have made a logical error in constructing your worksheet. However, sometimes the situation genuinely requires that the computer continues to evaluate the formulas until sufficient **convergence** has been reached. This is achieved by the OPTIONS "iteration:" field.

Column

The line of **cells** that stretches from the top of the **worksheet** to the bottom, as opposed to the **rows** that stretch from the left to the right side of the worksheet. There are 63 columns in a worksheet. There is also a COLUMN( ) **function**.

Command

1. How you tell Multiplan what you want it to do. There are 20 commands available.
2. There are also **sub-commands**, and **functions** which tell Multiplan what you want it to do.

Command Cursor

The **Command Cursor** is used to choose the Command that we are going to select in the **command lines** of the **control area** of the screen.

Command lines

The two lines at the top of the **control area** of the screen, which display the 20 Multiplan commands.

Concatenate

1. This means joining together different pieces of **text**.
2. You use it with the & symbol. It is also called **catenation** and you may also say that you will **catenate** two pieces of text. It only works on text, not on numbers.

Control area

1. The bottom four lines on the screen.
2. This is where you make things happen in the worksheet.

Convergence

A mathematical term referring to the fact that in some repeated calculations the difference between one calculation and the next gets progressively smaller.

Cursor

1.   The usual way that a computer tells you where you are about to enter information.

2.   The word pointer and the word cursor mean the same thing and in many manuals they are used interchangeably. In this book we make the following distinction:

Cell Pointer is used to show where we are making changes in the **Display Area**.
Command Cursor is used to choose the Command (or sub-command) that we are going to select in the **Command Lines**.
Edit Cursor is used to show us what we are going to edit in the Command, the value or the piece of text that appears in the **Command Line** while we are **edit**ing.

Default

1.   Usually means what the computer assumes that you want unless you tell it otherwise.

2.   In Multiplan it means the **alignments, format** codes and column widths that *you* choose for the entire **worksheet**, and can be superseded by other alignments, format codes and column widths for individual cells in the worksheet.

Delete

1.   To remove something.

2.   In Multiplan you may DELETE one, or more than one, rows or columns in one command. If you are deleting rows you may restrict it to some columns within those rows. Similarly if you are deleting columns you may restrict it to some rows within those columns.

Depend

1.   In Multiplan this refers to the relationship between worksheets that are **link**ed together.

2.   A summary sheet that gets its values from other sheets is said to depend, or be dependent, on them.

Direction key

In this book we use the term direction key to refer to a number of useful keys in Multiplan. We avoid directly naming them since they differ on various computers in order to take advantage of individual keyboards. The HELP KEYBOARD sub-command will show you which keys to use on your machine. As a standard the IBM Personal Computer keys are identified in this list:

move cursor left	left arrow
move cursor right	right arrow
move cursor up	up arrow
move cursor down	down arrow
move page up	Pg Up
move page down	Pg Dn
Move page left	Control and left arrow
Move page right	Control and right arrow
Home (in this window)	Home
End	End
Home to R1C1	Control and Pg Up

Directory

A list of all the Multiplan worksheets, also known as **files**, kept on the disk you are working on. You get the opportunity to look at it in the TRANSFER LOAD and TRANSFER DELETE sub-commands.

Display area

The top 20 lines of the screen where you get a window into your **worksheet**. You should not confuse this with the worksheet itself, which may be larger than what you can see on your screen at the moment.

Edit

1.   Editing in computers means changing something that you have entered into the computer previously.
2.   With the EDIT Command you can change both:

A command; and
the contents of a cell.

You may edit the contents of a cell in the ALPHA and the VALUE command, any command while you are still keying it in (that is before you have entered it) and any **proposed response** before you accept it.

Edit Cursor

The **Edit Cursor** is used to show us what we will edit in the Command, the value or the text that appears in the **command line** while we are editing.

Enter

1.   The word enter means putting information into the computer.

2.   When you have finished entering the information at the keyboard you press the 'Return' key. On some computers this may be called the 'Enter' key, or the 'Execute' key.

Exponential

1.   A term used in Mathematics. Mathematicians often refer to a value in terms of its relationship to the number 10. For instance, the number 10 is 10 to the power of 1, the number 100 is 10 to the power of 2, and 1000 is 10 to the power of 3. The small number against the large number is known as the **exponent**.

Number	Power of	Mathematical Notation
10	1	10^1
100	2	10^2
1000	3	10^3

2.   You do this in the format code **field** of the FORMAT Command because you can display larger numbers in a smaller column width. For instance, 10 million is expressed as 1E+06 when the format code of Exp has been used.

Extended entry

When entering a whole series of **values** and/or pieces of **text** you can speed up the process by not pressing 'Return', but instead moving straight on to the next cell into which you are going to **key** in the next item. This process is known as **extended entry**. You come out of it by cancelling the command in the **command line**.

External

Used in Multiplan to describe a worksheet other than the **active** worksheet.

Field

You enter the responses of the commands into fields, answering the questions that Multiplan poses. For instance, in COPY RIGHT you have to put replies to the "no of cells:" and "starting at:" fields.

File

1.   In computers collections of data are known as **files**. You could refer to an Accounts File or a Name and Reference File.

2.   The name that we give to each worksheet is also known to the computer's operating system as a **file**. This term arises in the messages that you get when entering the TRANSFER SAVE and TRANSFER DELETE sub-commands. You would also need to know the word if you were using the Multiplan worksheet as part of some data processing application.

Filename

The term used by your computer's operating system to mean the same thing as a worksheet. However, although all worksheets are filenames, not all filenames are worksheets.

FORMAT

In Multiplan the word 'format' is used in two different ways. These are:

FORMAT command, which controls how we display contents of cells.

Format code which is one of the **fields** of the FORMAT command.

Both are described below.

FORMAT

1.   The FORMAT command controls how the information in the computer is displayed either on the screen or on the printer.
2.   In Multiplan this means that we can determine the column width, the alignment, the format code and the number of decimal places. All this is explained on page 60, but remember you have formats in order to see what is in the computer in a form that is convenient to you. The FORMAT command never changes the internal representation of your information, the functions concerned with data representation, such as ROUND and INTEGER, always do. A good way of understanding what FORMAT does is to think of it as a display capability.

Format Code

The Format Code is one of the three **field**s of the FORMAT CELLS and the FORMAT DEFAULT CELLS sub-command. This one controls whether the cell is displayed as an integer, fixed decimal number, etc.

Formula

1.   The way you tell the computer to calculate the answer that you want. The rules for expressing it are much the same in Multiplan as they are in Mathematics.
2.   There is no command which enters a formula directly. You enter it as part of a VALUE command or its equivalents. These appear in this guide under the heading of VALUE. Every formula is recalculated every time you key in something new, unless you turn off **recalculation**. The rules for evaluating a formula will be obvious to anyone familiar with **BASIC**.

FUNCTION

The word 'function' has two different meanings in Multiplan:

Function, as a word on its own.

Function Keys, which are on your keyboard.

Both are explained below.

Function

1.   A **Function** is a **formula** that has already been worked out for you. There are 42 different functions available. They are all listed on page 23.
2.   You enter a function as a value or as part of a formula. You always have **parentheses** at the end of a function, even if no **argument** is needed.

Function key

Depending on your make of computer you have function keys to enable you to do something in one key stroke. For example, on the IBM Personal Computer you use Function Key 9 to move one character to the left while you are editing. Check in your manufacturer's handbook for details of your own function keys, or use the HELP KEY-BOARD feature. You do that by pressing 'H' for 'Help', followed by 'K' for 'Keyboard'.

General

1.   Used in the FORMAT command. This will interest advanced Multiplan users.
2.   **General** is a valid response for both the **Alignment Code** and the **Format Code** of the FORMAT command. It is similar, but not identical, to the **Default** code. The difference is that any defaults that you enter yourself will take precedence over the General codes, which are the ones that Multiplan suggests.

Help

Very structured information is available at the screen itself to guide you through the rules of Multiplan. You may have problems with its mathematical terminology. Once you have mastered Multiplan, you should be able to benefit from looking up an individual fact using this command.

Highlight

The way in which things can be emphasized for you on the screen. Instead of the symbols being colored against a black background you get the symbol in black against a colored background.

QUICK REFERENCE GUIDE

Inactive

The opposite of **Active**. Refers to the part that you are not looking at just now. For more information see 'Active'.

Insert

1.   To place something between two other things.
2.   In Multiplan you may INSERT one, or more than one, rows or columns in one command. If you are inserting rows you may restrict it to some columns within those rows. Similarly if you are inserting columns you may restrict it to some rows within those columns.

Integer

A whole number: one without any decimals in it.

Intersection

1.   Where a row meets a column is called an **intersection**.
2.   You may express groups of cells as **intersection**s of **range**s, or as **range**s of **intersection**s. You use an intersection in a formula or in response to a **command** or **sub-command**.

Iteration

1.   This term is used to describe what happens when Multiplan needs to repeat the same calculation automatically. This will interest the advanced Multiplan user.
2.   Multiplan has the capability of performing calculations that lead to **convergence**, or closer approximations to the required answer.

Justify

1.   Refers to two of the **alignment** codes in the FORMAT command. They are left justified and right justified, meaning that the cell's contents are hard against the left or right side of the cell.
2.   Remember that this refers only to the appearance of the cell's contents: the computer holds it in its own way.

Key

When you **enter** information into the computer, this is described by computer people as saying that you **key** it in.

Link

1.   In Multiplan we can **link** together two things: windows and worksheets.
2.   Linking **Windows** means that when we move the cell pointer in one window, the information moves in both windows in harmony with one another.

    Linking **Worksheets** means being able to use the information from one worksheet in another.

LOAD

If you are starting a Multiplan session using a worksheet that you have SAVEd on another occasion they you must LOAD it back in. This will ensure that you will get it back in exactly the same form that it was in when you saved it.

Logical function

Certain of the functions that we use in Multiplan allow us to cause decisions to be made according to the current values of the data. These are called Logical Functions.

Menu

1.   A menu is a list from which you can make a choice.
2.   You make your choice either by moving the **Command Cursor** to the position of the item in the menu or by pressing the initial letter of that menu item. The Command Cursor is always set in position to select a likely menu choice. This is called the **proposed response**.

Model

The term 'model' is often used in Multiplan manuals and means exactly the same as **worksheet**. The two terms can be used interchangeably. In this book we always refer to a worksheet.

Modulo

1.   A mathematical term. Also known as modulus.
2.   In Multiplan the function which returns the remainder that you would get when you divide the first argument in the function with the second. The function is called MOD.

Name

1.   The ability to **reference** a cell or group of cells makes Multiplan a more useful system. With a little care you can make a **formula** explain itself in English.
2.   A cell's name is quite independent of its contents. They may be the same or they may be different: it doesn't matter. A name is not visible on the screen but you may retrieve it by using the direction key.

Nesting

When one **function** uses another function as one of its **arguments**, this is called nesting them because one appears inside the other.

Operator

1. An operator is a mathematical term for the symbols like + and −.
2. The full list of Multiplan operators and their meanings is as follows:

Symbol	Meaning	Where Used
+	Add	Formulas
−	Subtract	Formulas
*	Multiply	Formulas
/	Divide	Formulas
^	Exponentiation	Formulas
%	Percent	Formulas
.	Period	Formulas
&	Concatenator	Text Functions
( )	Parentheses	Formulas and Functions
>	Greater than	Logical operations
<	Less than	Logical operations
=	Equal to	Logical operations
,	Comma	Functions

OPTION

Note that in Multiplan the word **option** is used in four different ways:

The OPTIONS command.

As a sub-command in the FORMAT command.

As a sub-command in the PRINT command.

As a sub-command in the TRANSFER command.

The uses are, of course, completely different.

OPTIONS

1. A collection of four quite different choices which affect the worksheet as a whole. The reason they are all grouped together is because this helps to keep the total number of commands down to a manageable 20.

2.   The four fields grouped together under the OPTIONS command are:

Recalc, which is mentioned in this guide.
Mute, which lets you prevent the computer from making beeping noises when you make a mistake.
Iteration, which is mentioned in this guide.
Completion test at, which is covered on page 75.

Page

A page is a whole screen's worth of information. So if we **scroll** down a page we see the next whole screen underneath the current screen. We can do the same thing in all the other three directions.

Parameter

This is the name that Multiplan uses for your reply to a field in a command. For example, a cell or group of cells is a parameter. The term is used in some of the messages that appear in the Message Line of the Control Area. The 'Illegal Parameter' message that you would get if you entered a non-existent row or column number is an example.

Parentheses

The symbols (and) that logically hold its contents together. Used in formulas and functions.

Pointer

1.   The usual way that a computer tells you where you are about to enter information.
2.   The word 'pointer' and the word 'cursor' mean the same thing and in many manuals they are used interchangeably. In this book we make the following distinction:

Cell Pointer is used to show where we are making changes in the **Display Area**;
Command Cursor is used to choose the Command (or Sub-command) that we are going to select in the **Command Line**s.
Edit Cursor is used to show us what we are going to edit in the Command, the value or the piece of text that appear in the **Command Line** while we are **edit**ing.

Pointing

The term used in this book to describe the action of entering a Reference, not by keying it in, but by using the Cell Pointer to enter the information instead. This concept is fundamental to Multiplan's ability to provide quick, intuitive answers to everyday problems.

Prepared Response

In some manuals the term 'Prepared Response' is used instead of **Proposed Response**. They mean exactly the same thing. In this book we use the term 'Proposed Response'.

Prompt

1.   Term used to describe the situation where the computer is waiting for you to enter the next piece of information and indicating this fact to you.
2.   In Multiplan the prompts always appear in the Message Line.

Proposed Response

Multiplan requires **responses** to the **fields** which appear in most commands. Where possible a response is proposed which, if correctly anticipating what you want, can be simply accepted. This saves time.

Prototype

Term used in this book to describe the worksheet that you create, *not* to use, but to SAVE in order to produce new copies which are then used. The reason for doing so is that in this way you only have to create your worksheet once.

Range

1.   A group of cells that are all adjacent to each other.
2.   The range will be in the shape of a rectangle with a fixed number of rows and a fixed number of columns on each side. A range is shown by the use of the colon, :, symbol. For example R15C20:R25C30 describes the rectangle of which the top left is Row 15 Column 20 and the bottom right is Row 25 Column 30. You use a range in a formula or in response to a **command** or **sub-command**.

Recalculate

1.   This is the automatic recalculation of every formula in the worksheet every time you key in something new. When you first start a new worksheet Multiplan sets automatic recalculation.
2.   In a large worksheet it is advisable to switch off this feature, using the recalc sub-command of the OPTIONS command. This will speed up your work. You can then cause recalculation to take place under your own control by using the Recalculate **Function Key**. You can also switch automatic recalculation on again by use of the same OPTIONS command.

Reference

1.   The way in which you tell Multiplan what cell or group of cells you wish to use.
2.   A reference to a cell or group of cells will consist of an **intersection**, or a **range** or a **union**, or any combination of these.

Relative reference

1.   This is the way of referring to a cell by counting its distance from the **active cell**. If the **cell pointer** is at Row 10 Column 10, then Row 9 Column 11 is expressed by Multiplan as R[−1]C[+1].
2.   The reason that we use **relative reference**s is that when we COPY a formula over a group of cells the same relative reference will be valid in the other cells to which we COPY it, saving a great deal of work. This is therefore the opposite of **absolute reference**s, where the reference remains the same in all the cells to which we COPY it.

But this relative reference also gets renumbered along with everything else that is involved whenever you modify the worksheet by INSERT, DELETE or MOVE. All the relative references, and the absolute ones too, get recalculated to what they should be.

Response

1.   How you reply to the 'question' that Multiplan has asked you.
2.   This could be one of the following:

    A **reference**.
    A **row** or **column** number.
    A **name**.
    The **text** that is required.
    The permitted list of **sub-commands** or codes.

The prompt in the Message Line will tell you which of the above things you should enter. Wherever possible, Multiplan suggests the **proposed response**.

Returns

1.   The term is used to mean getting a result.
2.   The term is used in particular when we talk about **functions**. For example, we say that SQRT(reference) returns the square root of the number in the reference.

QUICK REFERENCE GUIDE

Row

The line of **cell**s that stretches from the left of the **worksheet** to the right, as opposed to the **column**s that stretch from the top to the bottom of the worksheet. There are 255 rows in a worksheet.

Scroll

To cause the screen's view of the worksheet to move in one of the four directions (up, down, left or right). There are keys available to enable you to move a column or row, or a page, in any one of the four directions.

Session

1.   In this book we use the term 'session' to mean all the work we do from the time that we enter Multiplan until we leave it, irrespective of how many worksheets we have LOADed, SAVEd or RENAMEd.
2.   When we move from one worksheet to another in a session we lose all the normal FORMAT **default**s, but keep all the options from the OPTIONS, FORMAT, PRINT and TRANSFER commands.

Set

A mathematical term for a group of things belonging together.

Sheet

Another way of referring to a **worksheet**. In this book we always call it a worksheet.

Spreadsheet

A way of referring to a **worksheet**. So called because when we use them we spread out the information across the rows and columns. In this book we always call it a worksheet.

Status line

The bottom line of the screen and of the Control Area. It displays from left to right following pieces of information:

The position of the **Cell Pointer** at the start of the current command.
The contents of the current cell or the formula if there is one.
The percentage of space free for enlarging the **active** worksheet.
The name of the **active** worksheet.

String

A term used by computer people to refer to a group of characters that varies in length and may contain any characters, particularly alphabetic characters. Since this book is not written for computer people, we just call it **text**.

Sub-command

The effective number of commands is considerably greater than the 20 that appear in the **Command Lines** of the Control Area of the Screen. Many of the Commands themselves have up to four different **sub-commands**, which enable you to make them more specific.

Support

1.   In Multiplan this refers to the relationship between worksheets that are **link**ed together.

2.   The supporting worksheet is the one that provides the information for the sheet, for example a summary sheet, that **depend**s on it.

Symbolic

A term used to describe the format your worksheet will have in order to communicate with other computer systems.

Text

1.   The content of a cell that is neither numeric nor a formula. In the manuals it may be called a **string**. In this book the word 'text' is used instead.

2.   You cannot operate on text in a **formula** but you can **concatenate** it. Multiplan has some powerful functions to enable us to control the way that pieces of text are displayed. These are called text functions.

Union

1.   A way of referring to groups of cells. This will interest advanced Multiplan users. The use of the word is derived from mathematics.

2.   A union is a list. So if you COPY FROM a cell to three others which are not adjacent you could give the **response** to the "to cells:" field as R15C27,R18C27,R21C27. A union is indicated by the use of commas. You use a union in response to a **command** or a **sub-command**.

VALUE

There are three uses in Multiplan of the word value. These are:

The VALUE command.

The VALUE function.

Value, with the meaning of what is put in a cell.

All are explained below this line.

VALUE

The command which enters numeric information straight into a cell from the keyboard. Exactly the same result is achieved by the use of the symbols:

```
=
+
(
any numeric digit
```

They are all recognized by Multiplan as meaning the start of some numeric information.

VALUE( )

The VALUE( ) function converts into numeric form a piece of text which has characters which *can* form a number. You may want to use it when extracting part of a date field.

Value

A **value** can be either:

Keyed in under a VALUE command or as described immediately above.

The result of a calculation controlled by a **formula**.

Variable

A variable is a term used by computer people to mean something that can change during the course of the computer's operation.

Vector

1.   A mathematical term which describes, for example, the speed and direction of an airplane.

2.   In Multiplan this refers to a line of adjacent cells. The line may be horizontal or vertical but may only be one cell wide. It may be a whole row or a whole column. Multiplan recognizes a vector when you have **name**d one. Then if you use further NAME commands the proposed response will offer a vector which is similar in shape to your last vector.

Version

Multiplan has different **versions**. You can discover which version you have by entering the OPTIONS command and then selecting no sub-commands but just pressing 'Return'. You will see the version number displayed in the Message Line of the control area.

Window

1.   A window enables us to get a view of a particular part of the total worksheet. The screen can support a maximum of eight windows.

2.   The WINDOW command is important for the advanced use of Multiplan since it enables you to compare different parts of the worksheet at the same time. It saves you time and is also useful when you are showing your workings on the screen to someone else.

Window marker

The # symbol followed by a number identifies the **window** that you are looking at. It is one of the three highlighted areas on your screen.

Word

In Multiplan this refers to a character, or more usually a group of characters, that belong logically together in a command. The term is used when we **edit** a command, and speeds up the editing process. In the following example, there are 12 different words:

R[+2]C[−3]+(R14C23∗Taxation)−SUM(R27C20:29)

The 12 words are:

1.	R[+2]C[−3]	Relative Reference
2.	+	Operator
3.	(	Operator
4.	R4C23	Absolute Reference
5.	∗	Operator
6.	Taxation	Name
7.	)	Operator
8.	−	Operator
9.	SUM	Function
10.	(	Operator
11.	R27C20:29	Range
12.	)	Operator

Each time the LEFT WORD or WORD RIGHT function keys are used you will highlight the next word in the direction that you have chosen.

Worksheet

The worksheet is the grid of **row**s and **column**s in which we work. It is also known as a **sheet** and a **spreadsheet**. In this book it is known as a worksheet.

INDEX

The most important reference for any entry appears in **bold** print.